CAMBRIDGE LIBRARY COLLECTION

Books of enduring scholarly value

Philosophy

This series contains both philosophical texts and critical essays about philosophy, concentrating especially on works originally published in the eighteenth and nineteenth centuries. It covers a broad range of topics including ethics, logic, metaphysics, aesthetics, utilitarianism, positivism, scientific method and political thought. It also includes biographies and accounts of the history of philosophy, as well as collections of papers by leading figures. In addition to this series, primary texts by ancient philosophers, and works with particular relevance to philosophy of science, politics or theology, may be found elsewhere in the Cambridge Library Collection.

Hobbes

At the age of eighty-four, Thomas Hobbes (1588–1679) wrote an autobiography in Latin elegaics. Unsurprisingly, it was not as widely read as his two great philosophical works, *Leviathan* and *Behemoth*, in which he laid out a set of sociopolitical theories that enraged many of the philosophers and moralists of Europe. In this comprehensive biography, first published in 1904, Sir Leslie Stephen (1832–1904) charts the character and changes of Hobbes' thinking, from the scholasticism of his early Oxford education, to his later devotion to geometry and deductive science. With an emphasis on personal influences, Stephen sets Hobbes and his work in the historical context of Hobbes' often difficult patrons, the Civil War, and the Restoration, providing an insight into the life of the eminent philosopher and into the tenets of early twentieth-century biographical writing. An interesting text for students of both philosophy and English literature.

Cambridge University Press has long been a pioneer in the reissuing of out-of-print titles from its own backlist, producing digital reprints of books that are still sought after by scholars and students but could not be reprinted economically using traditional technology. The Cambridge Library Collection extends this activity to a wider range of books which are still of importance to researchers and professionals, either for the source material they contain, or as landmarks in the history of their academic discipline.

Drawing from the world-renowned collections in the Cambridge University Library and other partner libraries, and guided by the advice of experts in each subject area, Cambridge University Press is using state-of-the-art scanning machines in its own Printing House to capture the content of each book selected for inclusion. The files are processed to give a consistently clear, crisp image, and the books finished to the high quality standard for which the Press is recognised around the world. The latest print-on-demand technology ensures that the books will remain available indefinitely, and that orders for single or multiple copies can quickly be supplied.

The Cambridge Library Collection brings back to life books of enduring scholarly value (including out-of-copyright works originally issued by other publishers) across a wide range of disciplines in the humanities and social sciences and in science and technology.

Hobbes

LESLIE STEPHEN

CAMBRIDGE UNIVERSITY PRESS

Cambridge, New York, Melbourne, Madrid, Cape Town,
Singapore, São Paolo, Delhi, Mexico City

Published in the United States of America by Cambridge University Press, New York

www.cambridge.org
Information on this title: www.cambridge.org/9781108047654

© in this compilation Cambridge University Press 2012

This edition first published 1904
This digitally printed version 2012

ISBN 978-1-108-04765-4 Paperback

ENGLISH MEN OF LETTERS

HOBBES

ENGLISH MEN OF LETTERS

HOBBES

BY

SIR LESLIE STEPHEN

LONDON: MACMILLAN & CO., LIMITED
NINETEEN HUNDRED AND FOUR

CONTENTS

HOBBES

CHAPTER I

LIFE

THE biographer of the present day knows not whether
to envy or to pity his predecessors in the seventeenth
century. The increased advantages bring responsi-
bilities. The materials available were formerly of
manageable bulk ; nor was it thought necessary to
emulate scientific procedure by minutely investigating
a man's "environment" and tracing all the influences
which moulded his character or the character of his
ancestors. Thomas Hobbes, of Malmesbury, author
of the *Leviathan,* was the most conspicuous English
thinker in the whole period between Bacon and Locke,
and his long career, described on the modern scale,
would certainly have filled at least a couple of portly
volumes. The actual accounts fill only a few pages.
They tantalise the reader by many glimpses of a very
interesting personality. Yet, brief as they are, they
give perhaps as distinct an impression of the main
outlines of a notable figure as could have been produced by far more elaborate detail.

Hobbes himself was obviously convinced—I have
reasons for hoping that his conviction was well founded

A

—that a distant posterity would thirst for information about him. At the age of eighty-four he wrote an autobiography in Latin elegiacs. Two years later Anthony Wood published his book upon the history and antiquities of the University of Oxford. Through John Aubrey, their common friend, he obtained for it an autobiographical notice from Hobbes. Unluckily Dr. Fell, Dean of Christchurch, who bore the expense of publishing, claimed also the right of editing the work. Hobbes's statement that he had spent a certain period *in scribendo librum, qui nunc non solum in Anglia sed in vicinis gentibus notissimus est nomine Leviathan* was amended by inserting *monstrosissimum* after *librum*, and *publico damno* before *notissimus*. Hobbes was informed of this and other changes in the same spirit, and printed a remonstrance. Fell replied (what it was hardly for him to say) that an old man, with one foot in the grave, ought not to trouble himself and the world about such trifles, and printed at the end of the book a contemptuous reply to *irritabile illud et vanissimum animal Malmesburiense*. The original auto-biography fortunately remains ; it was printed soon after Hobbes's death along with the poem, and a *Vitæ Hobbianæ Auctarium* (by a Dr. Blackbourne) contain-ing some further information. The Auctarium was founded upon the collections of Aubrey, made for the benefit of Wood's later book the *Athenæ Oxonienses*. Aubrey was a personal friend of Hobbes, who came from the same county, and did his best to anticipate Boswell, though his aspirations fell far short of such success.[1] From these and sundry incidental refer-

[1] Aubrey's *Brief Lives*, containing these notes, have been carefully edited by Mr. Andrew Clark. 1898.

ences, we derive such knowledge of Hobbes as we possess; and in his case, as decidedly as in that of any philosopher, a knowledge of the man is very important to a fair appreciation of the work.

In the year 1588 a Thomas Hobbes was vicar of Westport, adjoining Malmesbury, and of the neighbouring parish of Charlton. He married, we are told, "... Middleton of Brokinborough (a yeomanly family)": but with that information students of heredity must be content. The vicar was "one of the ignorant Sir Johns of Queen Elizabeth's time: could only read the prayers of the Church and the homilies, and disesteemed learning as not knowing the sweetness of it." Another anecdote declares that he was a "good fellow," and that after playing cards all Saturday night, he went to sleep in church, and in his dreams announced to the congregation that clubs were trumps. Mrs. Hobbes heard rumours of the Spanish Armada, and apparently thought that Malmesbury would be the natural "objective" of an invading force. The result was the premature birth of her son Thomas, early in the morning of the 5th of April 1588. According to Aubrey the time was well chosen, as the child's horoscope, like that of Oliver Cromwell, indicated future eminence. Hobbes himself says that he and terror were born twins. Characteristically he speaks of his timidity with a certain complacency, and to it he attributes his hatred of his country's foes and his love of peace, with the muses and friendly company. Not long after his birth his father, "a choleric man," was provoked on purpose at the church door by "a parson (which, I think, succeeded him at Westport)." So Hobbes the elder struck him and was

forced to fly for it. He retired to a vague region
"beyond London," and there disappears from history.
Mrs. Hobbes was left at Malmesbury with three
children, including John, Thomas's senior by two
years, and a daughter. Fortunately a childless uncle,
Francis Hobbes, glover and alderman of Malmesbury,
took charge of the deserted family. Thomas was sent
to school at Westport church at the age of four, where
he learnt reading and arithmetic. Thence he passed
to a school in Malmesbury, and afterwards to one kept
by a Mr. Latimer, "a good Grecian, and the first that
came into our parts hereabout since the Reformation."
Latimer delighted in his scholar, and used to teach him
with "two or three ingeniose youths more" till nine
in the evening. Under this excellent master, Hobbes
worked to such good purpose that at the age of fourteen he had translated the *Medea* of Euripides into
Latin iambics. He was "playsome enough," though he
had even then a "contemplative melancholinesse":
and he was nicknamed "the crow" on account of his
black hair.

The promise which he had shown induced his uncle
to send him to Magdalen Hall at Oxford. He
apparently began residence in the beginning of 1603
(when he would be just fifteen) but was not admitted
to his B.A. degree till February 1608. At Oxford he
can scarcely have fulfilled his uncle's expectations.
He was one of the many eminent men who acknowledge but a small debt of gratitude to their university.
Long afterwards (in his *Behemoth*) Hobbes intimates
that the parliamentary commissioners, for whom he
had otherwise little enough affection, did some good
by purging the university of men morally unworthy,

as well as of those opposed to them in theology.
Many parents, he says, had reason to complain that
their sons were allowed to fall into vicious practices,
and taught by incompetent tutors little older than
themselves. The discipline and the studies at the
Oxford of that period seem, in fact, to have been in
much need of reform. Hobbes, however, writing in
his old age, had other causes of quarrel with the
universities, which he had come to regard as the
strongholds of obscurantism; and it does not appear
that, while himself a student, his eyes had been open
to the evils which he afterwards recognised.

Magdalen Hall was, during the early part of the
century, the favourite resort of the Puritans. But
there is no symptom that Hobbes was at the time
either attracted or repelled by the religious views of
his teachers. His account of his studies suggests the
probable state of the case. He was admitted, he says,
to the class of logic, and listened eagerly to the discourse of his beardless teacher. He was put through
the regular *Barbara celarent*, learnt the rules slowly,
and then cast them aside, and was permitted to prove
things after his own fashion. Swift, long afterwards,
speaks in much the same way of his logical studies in
Dublin. Then he was taught physics; the tutor
explained that all things were composed of matter
and form; that "species," flying through the air,
impressed the eye and ear; and attributed much to
sympathy and antipathy. Hobbes found such things
above his understanding; but it did not apparently
occur to him till a later period that they were unintelligible because nonsensical. Like many other lads, in
fact, he found his lessons tiresome; and he returned to

reading the books of which he had already an imperfect knowledge. He took a particular pleasure in
maps of the world and the stars; he liked to follow
the sun in fancy, and to trace the voyages of the great
circumnavigators, Drake and Cavendish. "He tooke
great delight" as Aubrey says, "to goe to the book-
binders' shops and lie gaping on mappes"; but it does
not appear that the records of the Elizabethan sailors
inspired him with the usual boyish ambition of
running away to sea. Aubrey records one other
amusement. Hobbes told him, in order to prove the
sharp-sightedness of jackdaws, how he used to tie
"leaden-counters" with pack-thread, smeared with
bird-lime and baited with cheese parings. The jackdaws would "spy them at a vast distance up in the aire
and as far as Osney Abbey" and strike at the "baite."
Athletic sports had not yet organised idleness, but
Hobbes seems to have found sufficient excuses for not
attending lectures. The results of his university
career were so far negative; but an incident which
happened soon after his degree seems to show that
the authorities thought well of him: well enough, at
least—for such inferences are not always very safe—
to declare him fit to be employed by somebody else.
The principal of Magdalen Hall recommended him to
William Cavendish, afterwards first Earl of Devonshire, and Hobbes formed a connection with the
Cavendish family which was of vital importance to
his whole career.

The first conspicuous Cavendish, the Sir William
who was employed in the visitation of monasteries by
Henry VIII., and had certain pickings from their
estates, married Elizabeth, a rich heiress in Derby-

shire, generally known as "Bess of Hardwick." She
was an imperious lady, who induced her husband to
settle in Derbyshire, where she built great houses at
Hardwick and Chatsworth. She had determined, it
seems, not to die as long as she could build; and it
was only a hard frost, suspending her building operations, which induced her to leave the world in 1608 at
the age of ninety. She had before that time married
two other husbands, the last being the Earl of Shrews-
bury, the host or gaoler of Mary Queen of Scots. All
her fortune, however, went to her second son, William
Cavendish, who also inherited at a later period the
estates of his elder brother, and was thus one of the
richest men in England. In 1618 he became first
Earl of Devonshire, having bought the title for £10,000
from James I. In 1608, when Hobbes was leaving
Oxford, he was father of a son William, afterwards
second earl, two years younger than Hobbes. According to Aubrey, the younger William (possibly his
father), "had a conceit that he should profit more in
learning if he had a scholar of his own age to wait on
him than if he had the information of a grave doctor."
Hobbes became "his lordship's page, and rode a hunt-
ing and hawking with him and kept his privy purse."
The "learning" seems to have been neglected: Hobbes
almost forgot his Latin; but bought a few books,
especially a Cæsar, which he carried in his pocket and
read in the lobby "while his lord was making his
visits." Another note gives a rather unpleasant aspect
of Hobbes's first position. "His lord," says Aubrey,
"who was a waster, sent him up and down to borrow
money and to get gentlemen to be bound for him,
being ashamed to speak himself." Hobbes, we are

told, "took cold, being wet in his feet (then were no
hackney coaches to stand in the streets), and trod both
his shoes aside the same way" (whatever that may
indicate). Notwithstanding, adds Aubrey, he was
loved for his facetiousness and good-nature. Young
Cavendish had been married to Christiana, daughter of
Edward, Lord Bruce of Kinloss. James I., who had
been served by Lord Bruce in the negotiations with
Cecil which secured his accession to the throne, gave
the bride £5000. She was only twelve years and
three months old at her marriage, and the bridegroom,
who was eighteen, was, for the present, more in need
of a tutor than a wife.

In 1610 the two young men made the grand tour,
visiting France and Italy. No record of their adven-
tures is preserved, but Hobbes says that he brought
back some knowledge, both of the modern languages
and of men and manners in the countries visited. It
was the year in which Henry IV. fell by the knife
of Ravaillac ; Hobbes mentions the murder once or
twice in his works ; but it was so apt an illustration
of his view as to the relation between kings and priests
that no personal memory need be implied. He brought
back one lesson of importance. He discovered that
the scholastic doctrine, of which he had acquired a
smattering at Oxford, was everywhere treated with
contempt by the intelligent, and was passing out of
fashion. He continued to live with the pupil who
had now become a friend. For the next eighteen years
Hobbes was a member of the Cavendish family. These
years, he says, were by far the pleasantest of his life,
and still (that is when he was eighty-four) revisited
him in his dreams. His patron allowed him leisure

and provided him with books of all kinds for his
studies. There was no one, says Hobbes, in whose
house a man would less need a university. Having
thrown aside his philosophy, Hobbes began by rubbing
up his old classical knowledge. He read poets and
historians with the comments of grammarians, in order
to acquire the art of writing a clear Latin style, then
a matter of practical importance for a man of letters.
He does not mention another study which occupied
part of the time. Aubrey tells us that he repented
of having spent two years in reading romances and
plays, and often lamented this waste of time. It
might, as Aubrey suggests, "furnish him with copie
of words." Anyhow, he undertook another task
which, one can well believe, helped him to acquire
the clear and forcible style of his English writings.

This was his translation of Thucydides. He said
long after that he had learnt from Thucydides how
much wiser one man is than a body of men, and
meant to warn his countrymen against trusting
popular orators. It must be admitted that this
method of meeting democratic tendencies was decidedly roundabout. Few people could be expected
to read the translated book, and those who did, might
fail to draw the desired inference. Hobbes was probably crediting himself with intentions suggested by
later experience. The introductory remarks show his
admiration for the skill with which Thucydides has
made his narrative pregnant with wisdom without
digressing into lectures. He ridicules the ancient
critic who assumed that the "scope of history" should
be "not profit by writing truth, but delight of the
hearer as if it were a song." He could not have

offered better advice to some modern historians. Hobbes, we may suppose, was not very much impressed by the weighty political utterances of the great historian, but felt a certain congeniality to his own intellectual tendencies. Anyhow the attempt to straighten out Thucydides' tough sentences into clear English was as good practice as could be desired. Hobbes had not received such training as is generally requisite for fine scholarship, and Jowett, in his preface to his own version, says that his predecessor's work is very rough and inaccurate, and has been praised beyond its merits. I cannot dispute the verdict of so high an authority. My readers may judge from a short specimen. It is part of the passage containing Thucydides' reflections upon the seditions in Corcyra. They would have a special interest for the author of the *Leviathan*.

"And many and heinous things happened in the cities through this sedition, which though they have been before, and shall be ever as long as human nature is the same, yet they are more calm and of different kinds according to the several conjunctures. For in peace and prosperity as well cities as private men are better minded because they be not plunged into necessity of doing anything against their will. But war, taking away the affluence of daily necessaries, is a most violent master, and conformeth most men's passions to the present occasion. The cities therefore being now in sedition, and those that fell into it later having heard what had been done in the former, they far exceeded the same in newness of conceit both for the art of assailing, and for the strangeness of their revenges. The received value of names im-

posed for signification of things was changed into
arbitrary. For inconsiderate boldness was counted
true - hearted manliness; provident deliberation a
handsome fear; modesty, the cloak of cowardice; to
be wise in everything, to be lazy in everything. A
furious suddenness was reputed a point of valour. To
readvise for the better security was held for a fair
pretext of tergiversation. He that was fierce was
always trusty; and he that contraried such a one was
suspected. He that did insidiate, if it took, was a
wise man; but he that could smell out a trap laid, a
more dangerous man than he. But he that had been
so provident as not to need to do the one or the other,
was said to be a dissolver of society, and one that
stood in fear of his adversary. In brief, he that
could outstrip another in the doing of an evil act, or
that could persuade another thereto that never meant
it, was commended."

Such are the evils, Hobbes would have said, which
follow when men's passions are let loose by the
destruction or dislocation of a settled sovereign
authority. He did not, however, at present set forth
his own views, and the translation remained for some
time unpublished. The years that he passed with the
Cavendishes, the years so fondly remembered, must
have been in the main devoted to thinking and reading in the intervals of the duties, whatever precisely
they may have been, imposed upon him by his relation
to his patron. His position enabled him to make
acquaintance with some of the most famous men of
the day. When Aubrey first met him a few years
later (1634), his talk ran a good deal upon Ben Jonson
and Sir Robert Ayton. Jonson, of course, was then

the most far shining of literary lights; and though
Ayton, who was related to the wife of Hobbes's patron,
has fallen into obscurity, he was then regarded as an
eminent critic and poet. Hobbes submitted his
Thucydides to these two. A much more interesting
connection was that with Bacon. Aubrey tells some
anecdotes which suggest certain chronological difficulties. Bacon, he says, "used to contemplate in his
delicious walks at Gorhambury." When a notion
darted into his mind, he would have it set down by
one of his attendants, and he often said that Hobbes
was quicker than any one else at catching his meaning
and putting it down intelligibly. Aubrey says also
that Hobbes helped to translate some of Bacon's
essays, notably that upon the greatness of cities, into
Latin : the Latin translation was published posthu-
mously in 1636. Hobbes, too, is Aubrey's authority
for the familiar story of Bacon's death being caused by
the experiment of stuffing a fowl with snow. Bacon
knew something of Hobbes's patron, and there is
nothing improbable in the other statements. The
time at which the meetings took place was probably
between Bacon's loss of office in 1621 and his death in
1626. The amount of intercourse must be doubtful.

One point however is clear. Bacon and Hobbes
were alike in rejecting the old scholasticism, and in
being profoundly impressed by the early stages of the
modern scientific movement. But in other respects
the relation is one of contrast. Bacon's great aim was
to extend the physical sciences by systematising ex-
perimental methods. Hobbes, though he incidentally
notices one of Bacon's experiments, has, as Croom
Robertson put it, "nothing but scorn for experiment

in physics." His own method is essentially deductive, and he takes no notice of what is called "Baconian induction." Hobbes's political theories have no exact counterpart in Bacon. Bacon embodied in his various writings much statesmanlike reflection, showing the deep insight of a keen observer profoundly interested in the affairs of the day. Hobbes, as we shall see, also watched the political movement of the time, but as an outside spectator; and he constructs an abstract theory as dogmatically as his successor and, in some degree, his disciple, Rousseau. The contrast of style was well put by Sprat, in answer to Sorbiere, who had mentioned the personal relation, and inferred an intellectual affinity. "Bacon," he says, "is short, allusive, and abounding in metaphors: Hobbes, round, close, sparing of similitudes, but ever extraordinarily decent in them. The one's way of reasoning proceeds on particulars and pleasant images, only suggesting new ways of experimenting without any pretence to the mathematics. The other is bold, resolved, settled upon general conclusions, and in them (if we will believe his friend) dogmatical." Hobbes may doubtless have received from his intercourse with Bacon some impulse towards his philosophical enterprise, but as yet there is no proof of his having undertaken to be a philosopher at this early moment in his career, and the impulse, when it came, was derived from other sources. Other friendships, which I shall have to mention, may have begun at this period; but for the present Hobbes had made no attempt to impress the world, and would only be known to others than his immediate friends as the secretary of the Earl of Devonshire.

In 1626, on the death of the first earl, Hobbes's patron succeeded to the peerage, but died in June 1628. During the interval Hobbes wrote a Latin poem, giving an account of a short tour in the Peak, made in company with the second earl. It was, it appears, a new year's gift to his friend, who rewarded him with a present of £5. The *De Mirabilibus Pecci Carmen* begins with a description of the beauties of Chatsworth, and the early landscape-gardening of "Bess of Hardwick," where "art, dissimulating art," has produced sham rocks and streams and fountains. Then he describes the ride, in the course of which he and his companion see the seven wonders of the Peak :—Chatsworth itself, the cave called after the devil, Mam Tor, Eldon Hole, the hot spring, Pool's Cavern, and Buxton Well. Hobbes, it is needless to say, does not anticipate the Wordsworthian cult of Nature ; but he is a very good specimen of the early sightseer. Eldon Hole, it seems, was already famous in the days of Queen Elizabeth. The Earl of Leicester of that time caused a man to be let down into it hanging to a rope, and then to drop stones to estimate the remaining depth. When drawn up again he was too horror-struck to speak intelligibly, was seized with a frenzy, and died in a week. I regret to see that recent explorers have not spared the romance even of Eldon Hole. It is only two hundred feet deep, with an inner cave of less than a hundred. The party slept at Buxton, where they had two baths and a very poor supper (such descriptions are an essential part of all mountaineering literature), and returned next day to Chatsworth. The excursion was, we may guess, one of the incidents which revisited Hobbes in the dreams of his old age.

Unfortunately the poet, while describing the wonders, does not condescend to report the conversation of the travellers.[1]

The death of the second earl had serious effects for Hobbes. In the "Epistle Dedicatory" prefixed to the Thucydides, Hobbes tells the young heir that he is bound to dedicate his labour to "my master now in heaven." The panegyric upon the dead man which naturally follows is honourably free from the excessive adulation of such documents. Hobbes's sincerity is unmistakable. He speaks of the earl's liberality to himself, his good sense and freedom from factious motives. He gave sound advice and was "one whom no man was able to draw or justle out of the straight path of justice. Of which virtue, I know not whether he deserved more by his severity in imposing it (as he did to his last breath) on himself, or by his magnanimity in not exacting it to himself from others. No man better discerned of men: and therefore was he constant in his friendships, because he regarded not the *fortune* nor the *adherence* but the men, with whom also he conversed with an openness of heart that had no other guard than his own integrity and that *nil conscire*. To his equals he carried himself equally, and to his inferiors familiarly; but maintaining his respect

---

[1] De Quincey, in his Essay upon Murder as one of the Fine Arts, quotes from an anonymous tract of 1670 ("The creed of Mr. Hobbes examined"), by Thomas Tenison, afterwards archbishop. It describes a meeting with Hobbes at Buxton, to which place Hobbes's poem had attracted the author. Hobbes has a long dialogue with a student of divinity, and is thoroughly confuted. Tenison however states that the introductory circumstances as well as the dialogue are purely fictitious.

fully and only with the native splendour of his birth.
In sum, he was one in whom it might plainly be perceived that honour and honesty are but the same thing
in different degrees of persons." The earl had shown
some independence during his short tenure of the
peerage by opposing the Duke of Buckingham. He
had, however, spent his large revenues too lavishly and
been obliged to get a private act of Parliament to
enable him to sell some entailed estates. His death,
20th June 1628, was said to have been hastened by
"excessive indulgence in good living." Hobbes
naturally does not mention this in his dedication; but
he suffered from the consequences.

The widowed countess, left with three children,
the eldest son eleven years old, set about regulating
her affairs, as became her Scottish descent. She was
an intelligent and energetic woman, admired in later
years by Edmund Waller and others, and on friendly
terms with Hobbes. The retrenchments, however,
which she thought necessary, involved his leaving his
old situation, and he had to look out for other means of
support. He accepted the position of travelling tutor
to the son of Sir Gervase Clinton, of an old Notting-
hamshire family. A letter from Wotton to Sir
Thomas Wentworth (4th April 1628) mentions the lad :
" Pray tell him [Sir G. Clinton] that when he sent his
son hither [to Eton, of which Wotton was then provost]
he honoured, and when he took him away he wounded
us. For in this Royal Seminary we are in one thing
and only one like the Jesuits, that we all joy when we
get a spirit upon whom much may be worked." We
may hope, therefore, that Hobbes had a satisfactory
pupil. They were abroad for eighteen months. An

undated letter mentions an intended visit to Venice,
probably prevented by war. Hobbes was now forty, a
time by which a man's intellect is generally ripe and
his aspirations tolerably fixed. He had passed years
in quiet study, and must have been interested in the
political questions which were becoming daily more
pressing in England. He must, one supposes, have
had comparisons suggested to him by the state of
things in France, where Richelieu was building up the
great state which most nearly represented his own
ideal "Leviathan," while in the country of Machiavelli, he would be led to observe the famous constitution of Venice, admired by so many of his
contemporaries as the highest achievement of political
architecture, and would have his own thoughts about
the great spiritual power which now occupied the seat
of the Roman empire. Hobbes's method, however,
involves little appeal to observation of particular
events or to his own personal experience, however
deeply they may have impressed him. He tells us,
on the other hand, of one discovery which was certainly borne in upon him during this journey, while
another may probably belong to it or to his next visit
to the continent. The incidents might as well have
occurred at London as in Paris. The first is best
told by Aubrey: "Being in a gentleman's library
Euclid's *Elements* lay open, and 'twas the 47th *El.
libri I.* He read the proposition. 'By God,' sayd he,
'this is impossible'" (he would now and then swear by
way of emphasis, as Aubrey apologetically notes). "So
he reads the demonstration of it which referred him
back to such a proposition : which proposition he read.
That referred him back to another, which he also read.

Et sic deinceps that at last he was demonstratively
convinced of that truth. This made him in love with
geometry." The knowledge, it must be admitted, came
rather late, and the ignorance is not to the credit of
his early instructors. As I shall have to say, however,
the effect upon his later speculations was of singular
importance. The second incident, whenever it happened, was equally fruitful. He was at a gathering
of "learned men," where something was said about sensation. One of them asked, as in contempt, what was
sense ? Hobbes thereupon wondered how it happened
that men who took such pride in the title of "wise"
could be ignorant of the nature of their own senses.
Thinking over the matter himself, he remarked that
if all things were at rest or all moved alike, there
could be no difference of things and consequently no
sense. He inferred that the cause of all things must
be sought in the difference of their movements. This
again threw him back upon geometry, and led him to
what he took to be his great discoveries. Such is the
difference, is his comment, between those who seek for
truth by their own genius, and those who seek it by
consulting authority or for purposes of gain. Whatever may be thought of his principles, he is certainly a
remarkable instance of an active mind set at work by
remarks which others pass by as common-places. I
shall have to speak hereafter of the essential part which
these two doctrines played in his later speculation.[1]

[1] There are certain difficulties about the date of the conversation "with learned men": and the discovery by Dr.
Tönnies of a ms. treatise in Hobbes's hand, giving an early
version of his doctrine, rather complicates the question as to
the evolution of his thought. I need not, however, go into
these details. See Robertson, p. 35 n.

It is for the present enough to observe that we may consider Hobbes as engaged in the elaboration of his philosophy from this period. He had hitherto, after learning the futility of the Oxford scholasticism, been interested in literature and especially in the historians, with reference, no doubt, to the political questions of the time. He now took up philosophy again from the scientific and mathematical side, and elaborated the ambitious scheme of which I shall speak presently. It implied, as we shall see, that he cast aside authority and considered himself to be capable of founding a new system of thought by his own unaided genius. For a while, however, he had employment which must have occupied much of his time. In 1631 he was invited to return from Paris to superintend the education of the third Earl of Devonshire, the son of his old patron or pupil, now about fourteen years of age. He was beginning to be absorbed in his new studies, but accepted a task which would still leave him some leisure, and to which he thought himself bound by gratitude to the family. He taught the boy industriously, seeking to imbue him "with all such opinions as should incline him to be a good Christian, a good subject, and a good son." The lessons included Latin composition, astronomy, geography, logic, and law. An abstract of Aristotle's *Rhetoric*, which appears in his works, was dictated to the pupil in Latin. The boy was docile and intelligent, and in later years revered and protected his teacher. The recall of Hobbes by the countess shows that his discharge had not implied disapproval. In later years the son, upon coming of age, was dissatisfied with some of his mother's dispositions of the estate. Hobbes went into the matter with the son and helped to arrange terms of agreement. He persuaded the young man to give up the intention of legal proceedings, and to remain in his mother's house. In the document which records the result, he notes that he has not acted for a reward, but simply as discharging the duty of a faithful tutor. To this period belongs a correspondence with another member of the family, William Cavendish, Earl and afterwards Duke of Newcastle, son of a third son of "Bess of Hardwick," and first cousin therefore to the second Earl of Devonshire. The duke's claim to literary glory is founded upon his books upon horsemanship, though he also wrote comedies, and collaborated with his second wife, the famous and eccentric Margaret, in some of her voluminous plays. He was a man of considerable intelligence, who is said to have been a patron of Descartes and Gassendi, as well as of Hobbes. Hobbes writes to him in January 1633 about an expected work from Galileo, which he has endeavoured to procure for the earl in London. Later correspondence shows that Hobbes was employed in elaborating his philosophy and counting upon Newcastle's sympathy.

In 1634 Hobbes started for his third visit to the continent, accompanying his pupil on the usual grand tour. They were at Paris in October, and afterwards visited Italy, returning again to Paris. This tour marks Hobbes's first recognition by philosophical contemporaries. He was at Florence in April 1636, anxious, as he says in a letter, to read Heylin's *History of the Sabbath*, and Selden's *Mare Clausum*. At this time, too, he saw Galileo, who had lately made his famous recantation, and was living near Florence as a prisoner of the Inquisition. He was admitted to the friendship of the great man, whom he mentions in his books with profound respect. Not long afterwards, Galileo had another remarkable English visitor, John Milton. What he thought of them we unfortunately do not know; but each of them carried away characteristic impressions. During this whole journey Hobbes's mind was always employed upon one topic. Whether he was in a ship or a carriage or on horseback, he was meditating upon the nature of the world, and working out the idea which had struck him at that "meeting of learned men." There was, he held, but one real thing in the world, the basis of all that we falsely take to be things, and which are mere phantasms of the brain. The one reality is motion, and to study the modes of motion is therefore the necessary condition for all successful researches in science. Full of this thought, he reached Paris and communicated it to a remarkable man who approved and brought it to the notice of others.

Hobbes was fortunate in his new acquaintance. Marin Mersenne, a man of his own age, belonged to the Friars Minim of the Franciscan Order, and was living in a monastery near the Place Royale. Before leaving the college of La Flèche he had known Descartes, his junior by eight years, who had entered the same college and already shown his precocity. Some years later the acquaintance was renewed, and Mersenne encouraged Descartes to devote his life to study. He became Descartes's most trusted and ardent friend, and acted as his "plenipotentiary" when Descartes retired to Holland. He accepted his friend's doctrines, defended him against accusations of heterodoxy, attracted dis-

ciples, and effected reconciliations (when possible) with
enemies. Mersenne was himself on friendly terms
with thinkers of opposite schools. He had some
scientific ability, and had lately published a translation of Galileo's *Mechanics*, which made the author's
reputation in France. He appears to have been a man
of singular simplicity and kindliness of nature, and his
cell in the monastery became the place of meeting for
the savants of Paris, and for distinguished strangers.
He discharged, as Baillet (the biographer of Descartes)
put it, the same function in the republic of letters as
the heart discharges in the human body. Hobbes says
that his cell was preferable to all the schools of philosophers. The star of every art (he becomes quite
poetical in his enthusiasm) revolved round Mersenne
as the axis of its orbit. The little constellation of
shining lights, who in those days were dispelling the
old darkness and revealing the foundation of modern
science, was widely scattered, and often its component
stars were isolated. They had, it is true, the advantage of a common language; but there were no
scientific societies or journals, and to facilitate their
intercourse, and make each aware of what was being
done by others, was a valuable service for which
Mersenne was especially qualified. Hobbes was welcomed by him, and began, as he puts it, "to be
numbered among the philosophers." He thus received
a kind of honorary diploma entitling him to speak
with authority. He was not loath to accept the
position. That a man who had not seen Euclid till he
was forty, and had only taken up philosophy at a later
period, should claim before he was fifty to be on terms
of equality with the leaders of thought throughout the

whole range of human knowledge would now seem preposterous. But physical science was still in its germ, and philosophy, making a fresh start, was pronouncing study of the old doctrines to be rather an encumbrance than an advantage. The field to be covered was so small that Hobbes, like Bacon or Descartes, might claim to survey the whole intellectual world and lay down the law upon things in general.

Henceforth Hobbes was a man with a mission. He had still to elaborate the details of his creed, but the first principles were already clear to him. Before dealing with his career as the expounder of a philosophy, I may make one remark suggested by his alliance with Mersenne. Hobbes's ethical theories have been condemned as egoistical and cynical; and it might be inferred that these unpleasant qualities were the reflection of his personal character. Of the ethics I shall speak hereafter; but the inference as to character requires, to say the least, very important reservations. It would be altogether unjust to set down Hobbes as a man of cold nature. Whether he was a man to make any romantic sacrifice to friendship may indeed be doubted. Retired philosophers may congratulate themselves that they are seldom exposed to such trials, and in Hobbes's life the case did not occur. But everything goes to show that he was a man of kindly if not of ardent affections. Few men appear to have won so many friends or to have retained them so permanently. His long connection with the Cavendish family proves the existence of a mutual esteem creditable to both sides. His language about Mersenne is as warm and sincere as his language about his early friend the second earl. The friendship with

Mersenne led to an equally warm friendship with
Gassendi and with many distinguished men. Hobbes
got into plenty of controversies, and the philosopher was
assailed more bitterly than any thinker of his time. It
is the more remarkable that no serious imputation is
made upon the man. Clarendon, when confuting his
abominable doctrines, declares that Hobbes was one of
his oldest friends, and emphatically asserts the personal
esteem entertained by himself and others for his antagonist. Hobbes seems to have been personally attractive
to everybody whom he met. He was a pleasant companion, and clearly had wit enough to be acceptable in
every circle. But no spiteful sayings are attributed to
him, and, although he quarrelled over geometry, he
excited no personal antipathy. Certainly we cannot
claim for him the posthumous affection which is
bestowed upon men of the heroic type like his contemporary Milton, or of the saintly type like Archbishop Leighton. But neither of those eminent persons made any mark in philosophical speculation.
We must admit the excellence for its own purpose of
more than one type. A man who is above all to be a
cool reasoner and to shrink from no conclusion forced
upon him by his logic, is a very valuable person, and
may be forgiven if his spiritual temperature does not
rapidly rise to boiling-point and obscure his clearness
of vision. Hobbes, if one may venture to say so, had
probably quite as much benevolence as was good for a
metaphysician.

Hobbes returned to England in 1637, and began at
once to compose his exposition. He was still employed by his pupil, who came of age in 1638, and in
1639 he was helping to arrange matters between the

young earl and his mother. To this time also must be
chiefly referred his intercourse with the remarkable
group, affectionately commemorated by Clarendon.
Its most attractive member was Lord Falkland, who
has won the regard of posterity by the charm of his
character rather than by any special achievement.
He lived at Tew, a few miles from Oxford, and, according to Clarendon's account, kept open house for all the
most distinguished members of the university. Among
the men who could drop in and make free use of his
table and library, were the divines, Sheldon and
Morley, afterwards bishops, and Hammond and
Chillingworth, who died before the Restoration, while
occasional wits and poets came over from London.
Whether Hobbes was ever of the party does not
appear. Falkland, however, according to Aubrey, was
"his great friend and admirer"; and besides Clarendon himself, one who afterwards gave substantial
proof of his regard, was Sidney Godolphin, a poet of
some reputation. If Hobbes joined the circle, he
would not find its opinions altogether congenial.
There was not much love lost between him and actual
or potential bishops; and Morley, Sheldon, and Hammond would be too strictly orthodox for his taste.
Falkland, Chillingworth, and their friend, the "ever
memorable" John Hales, represented a rationalising
movement within the church, and were suspected of
"socinianism." Of one of them, Hobbes made a characteristic remark to Aubrey. He commended Chillingworth for a very great wit: "But, my God," said he
(swearing by way of emphasis again), "he is like some
lusty fighters that will give a damnable back-blow now
and then on their own party!" Chillingworth's

vigorous logic shows an intellect congenial to that of
Hobbes himself; but Hobbes would no doubt think
that his rationalism logically led to opinions lying
beyond the borders of orthodoxy. In politics there
was a similar relation. Falkland was taken by Matthew
Arnold as embodying the sweet reasonableness which
condemns extremes on all sides. We hear him still
"ingeminating peace" after swords were drawn—a
most amiable but unfortunately a rather futile proceeding. He and Clarendon were constitutionalists,
opposed equally to the extreme claims of king and
parliament, though when it became necessary to take a
side, they preferred the royalist cause. A characteristic passage in the *Behemoth* speaks of the bad advice
given by men—Hobbes declines to revive old bitterness by giving their names—who believed in "mixed
monarchy," which in reality is pure "anarchy."

Hobbes might be contrasted with Falkland. Though
Falkland was moderate enough to see faults on both
sides, he was ready to fight and indeed to throw away
his life for the side which was least to blame. Hobbes
had no doubt upon political or any other questions;
but he was quite clear that he would fight for neither
side. Fighting, he might fairly urge, had never been
his trade, and he was clearly too old to take it up.
Meanwhile political controversy was raging with in-
creasing bitterness, and must have occupied the
thoughts of every one with whom Hobbes might con-
verse. No doubt eager discussions were going on in
the Falkland circle. Hobbes conceived that he had
something to say of considerable importance, and probably exaggerated the attention which logic was likely
to receive in the disturbed atmosphere.

The exaction of ship-money in 1637 had led to the famous proceedings against Hampden, and the decision against him in 1638. The Scots were becoming restive under the imposition of the new liturgy ; they were swearing to the covenant in 1638; and in 1639 a Scottish army was successfully resisting the king, and receiving the sympathy of the popular party in England. Charles was forced to appeal to a parliament in April 1640, after eleven years, during which that troublesome body had been suspended. Men were discussing fundamental political principles, and ready to settle them by an appeal to the sword. It was time, thought Hobbes, to speak out. He had formed and begun to execute a remarkable plan. He intended, like a sound logician, to lay down the first principles of all scientific inquiry, to apply them to what we should now call psychology, setting forth the laws of human nature, and finally to found upon this basis a science corresponding to modern sociology. He now dropped the first part and wrote a little treatise in two sections, omitting the first principles, but giving first a summary of his psychology, and secondly his political doctrine. The treatise was circulated in manuscript and occasioned much talk of the author. Had it not been for the dissolution of the Short Parliament, it would, as he thought, have brought him into danger of his life. The Long Parliament, however, which met in November, ready to fall upon Strafford, might find time also to deal with the author of this treatise.

Hobbes, "doubting how they would use him, went over into France the first of all that fled, and there continued eleven years, to his damage some thousands

of pounds deep." It does not appear how he arrived
at this estimate. Few other men would have prided
themselves on being the first to run away, and it may
be doubted whether it proved, as he apparently
thought, his foresight, or implied an erroneous appreciation of the danger. The treatise is undoubtedly a
remarkable book, and gives the pith of his most
characteristic teaching. Still he avoids so carefully
any direct reference to any passing event that it
might have failed to attract notice. Hobbes might
surely have given credit to members of parliament for
sufficient stupidity to overlook logical implications.
If indeed they thought him worth punishing, no weak
crotchet about liberty of the press would have re-
strained them. The House of Commons was quite
ready to suppress objectionable writers. Hobbes himself says he was preaching the same doctrine as Bishop
Manwaring. Manwaring had been a victim of the
parliament of 1628, for sermons attributing absolute
authority to the king. When the parliament was
dissolved the king had pardoned and preferred him,
and the Short Parliament found time to fall upon him
again and send him to the Tower. Hobbes's treatise
argues that the "sovereignty" is one and indivisible,
and necessarily carries with it the right to make peace
or war and to levy taxes. Sovereignty, as he truly
says, was then admitted to be in the king, and it
follows that Charles could raise ship-money or whatever taxes he pleased. If parliament were equal to
drawing that inference, and thought Hobbes's treatise
of sufficient importance, they would have little scruple
about applying the arguments directed against Manwaring.

Hobbes's political theory was fully formed before the outbreak of the war. He watched the events with interest, but of course knew beforehand that they would only confirm his theory. That result is sufficiently set forth in the *Behemoth*—a history of the period, written in 1668, to explain the causes of the rebellion. The book has a certain interest at this point in throwing some light upon Hobbes's sympathies when the war was actually raging. Hobbes was not yet a historical philosopher to the point of scientific impartiality. He too often, like many better historians, finds it enough to explain events by the wickedness of the other side. That agreeable theory is an excuse for not attempting to discover the causes of discontent; a wicked man wants no cause. He gives occasionally a quaint enough argument. The king's soldiers were as stout as their enemies, but could not fight so keenly "because their valour was not sharpened so with malice." To this he adds the additional reason that there were many raw London apprentices in the parliamentary army "who would have been fearful enough of death approaching visibly in glistening swords; but, for want of judgment, scarce thought of such death as comes invisibly in a bullet, and therefore were very hardly to be driven out of the field." Hobbes had clearly not been under fire.

He had plenty to say that is more to the purpose, and expressed with his usual terse and pointed style. One line of remark is characteristic. A letter to the Earl of Devonshire, in August 1641, discusses a petition against bishops. Hobbes thinks that it proves the existence of many abuses, and heartily approves of a proposal to give more authority to the laity. "Ministers," he thinks, "should minister rather than govern." Experience teaches that "the dispute between the spiritual and the civil power has of late, more than anything in the world, been the cause of civil wars in all places of Christendom." He already holds the view which becomes prominent in the *Behemoth.* He starts with a long comparison of the claims of the Papacy and their evil results; only at the end he remembers that, however many crimes the popes may have committed, they are scarcely to be accused of having prompted the Puritan revolt. The Papists, he has to explain, would not be sorry for disorders that might possibly clear the way for the restoring of the pope's authority. The Puritans are most clearly responsible. "After the Bible was translated in English, every man, nay every boy and woman, thought they spoke with God Almighty and understood what He said, when by a certain number of chapters a day they had read the Scriptures once or twice over." They lost their reverence for the bishops, and were supported by the gentry, who desired popular government in civil matters as non-conformists did in ecclesiastical. Thus supported, the presbyterian preachers went on to declaim against tyranny. They played the part of "right godly men as skilfully as any tragedian in the world." They took care indeed not to inveigh against the lucrative vices, such as lying, cozening, and hypocrisy, "which was a great ease to the generality of citizens and the inhabitants of market towns, and no little profit to themselves." "The inhabitants of market towns" were already fertile in the Stigginses of the period. Hobbes detests

the Presbyterians more than the Independents; for
the Presbyterian claimed a spiritual authority over the
State for his own church; still his preaching led to
the multiplication of sects. "There was no so
dangerous an enemy to the Presbyterians as this
brood of their own hatching." The Rump, he observes,
voted liberty of conscience to the sectaries and so
"plucked out the sting of presbytery," a feat which
was personally useful to Hobbes himself. Meanwhile
the established church had its faults. The clergy in
general thought that the pulling down of the pope
was the setting up "of them in his place." Their
doctrine of apostolical succession implied that their
"spiritual power did depend not upon the authority of
the king but of Christ himself." He admits that
Laud was a "very honest man," but intimates that he
was a very poor statesman for mixing state affairs
with his "squabblings in the university about free
will, and his standing upon punctilios concerning the
service book and its rubrics."

Though an absolutist in politics, Hobbes can cordi-
ally denounce persecution. "A state can constrain
obedience but convince no error, nor alter the mind of
them that think they have the better reason. Suppression of doctrines does but unite and exasperate:
that is, increase both the malice and the power of them
that have already believed them." Persecution results
from the desire of the spiritual power to enforce the
dogmatic systems learnt in the schools. "Religion
has been generally taken for the same thing with
divinity [that is, with metaphysical theology], to the
great advantage of the clergy." Though the translation of the Bible did mischief, he approves of it on the

whole. The Bible teaches good morality in the easiest words. The mischief resulted from the use of the Scriptures in controversies over mysteries. It is only when the State is subordinate to the Church that abstract dogmas will be enforced by law, and it is only in Christian countries that there have been wars of religion, because there men have been encouraged to wrangle and harangue upon such points. The introduction of this scholastic dogmatism is a main count in his indictment against the universities. "The universities have been to this nation as the wooden horse was to the Trojans." They are the "core of rebellion." It might have been said that the revival of classical literature was a point in their favour. But that only suggests another charge. They taught men to argue "for liberty out of the works of Aristotle, Plato, Cicero, and Seneca, and out of the histories of Rome and Greece"—not, it would seem, paying proper attention to Thucydides. Things will never be well till they are reformed and made to teach absolute obedience to the laws of the king "and his public edicts under the great seal of England": that is, as one of his opponents sneered, till the *Leviathan* has become the accepted text-book.

Hobbes on reaching Paris had renewed his old relations with Mersenne, and his first bit of work was a return to purely philosophical activity. Descartes had published his famous treatise on *Method* in 1637, and was now about to follow it up by the *Meditations*. Mersenne had submitted the book before publication to various learned men who were to offer criticisms which, with Descartes's replies, might be expected to throw light upon any obscurities in the new system.

Hobbes came just in time to join in this operation. He put certain objections briefly and bluntly, and they are of much interest as illustrating his own relation to Descartes. But they did not answer the intended purpose. Descartes had expected, and he more or less received from others, the rare and useful kind of criticism which comes from thinkers who are sufficiently in sympathy with their author to draw from him additional explanations of his thought and help him to round off and perfect his exposition. But Hobbes differed radically. The controversy very rapidly reached the point at which flat contradiction takes the place of friendly argument, and Descartes did not like contradiction for its own sake any more than any other philosopher. Instead of a partial ally he found a dogged opponent, and one who thought himself entitled to speak with fully equal authority. Descartes naturally became convinced that Hobbes was a very poor philosopher. There was not, he said, a single sound conclusion in the objections. Matters did not improve when Mersenne forwarded to Descartes certain objections to his *Dioptrique*. In order to secure a fair hearing, Mersenne concealed the fact that these objections also were made by Hobbes. Descartes did not suspect the little artifice, but did not like the new objections any better. He would, he said, have nothing more to do with the Englishman. At a later period Descartes admitted that Hobbes was a more competent writer upon political problems than upon metaphysical and mathematical questions, although his political principles were morally objectionable. He held that all men were wicked and gave them ground for wickedness. Hobbes on his side, according

to Aubrey, had a "high respect" for Descartes, but
thought that "his head did not lie for philosophy":
he ought to have confined himself to geometry. He
could not pardon him for writing against his conscience in defence of "transubstantiation in order to
please the Jesuits." This unsatisfactory encounter did
not long detain Hobbes. His interest in the political
issues of the civil war continued, and his thoughts
were for ten years "much or almost altogether
unhinged from the mathematics." The first result of
his meditations was the *De Cive* (1642), which is substantially a remodelling of the political part of the
"little treatise." It was written in Latin, by way
apparently of implying that it was intended for the
philosophical world of Europe, and only a small
number of copies was printed.

Hobbes then began the composition of his most
famous work, the *Leviathan*. This time he used his
native language, and meant, it is to be presumed, to
catch the attention of the politicians who were
remoulding the constitution of his own country. The
Leviathan, like the early treatise, covers the second
and third parts of his general plan, the first principles
being again postponed. It is always easy to supply
first principles when you have settled your conclusions.
One characteristic may be noted. In the first treatise
he had asserted his principle of the subordination of
the Church to the State. This argument, however,
was greatly expanded in the *De Cive*, and now in
the *Leviathan* fills a still larger space. For whatever
reason, Hobbes's antipathy to the claims of the spiritual
powers, whether Catholic or Presbyterian, had been
growing in intensity. The *Leviathan*, which Hobbes

hoped, and not without reason, would make an epoch in political speculation, was carefully and slowly written. Aubrey describes his method. "He walked much and contemplated ; and he had in the head of his staff a pen and ink horn ; carried always a note-book in his pocket, and as soon as a thought darted, he presently entered it into his book, or otherwise he might perhaps have lost it. He had drawn the design of the book into chapters, etc., so that he knew whereabouts it would come in." The composition took some years, during which, one would suppose, Hobbes must have been often in financial straits. Mersenne's failure to bring him into friendly relations with Descartes did not prevent the continuance of his own friendship. Another conspicuous member of the Mersenne circle, held to be only second to Descartes, was Gassendi. He settled in Paris as professor of mathematics in 1645, and became a warm friend. Hobbes called Gassendi the "sweetest-natured man in the world," and Gassendi expressed the highest ad-miration for Hobbes's writings. A less distinguished acquaintance, Sorbière, was rather a hanger-on than a member of the circle. He wrote books upon medical topics, and vainly tried to get patronage from the pope for his conversion from protestant error, but neither the pope nor other observers seem to have considered him as particularly edifying. Meanwhile he boasted of his friendship for Gassendi, whose life he wrote. He also professed admiration for Hobbes, who allowed him to publish a definitive edition of the *De Cive* at Amsterdam. It was delayed until 1647, when it came out accompanied by two most enthusi-astic letters of commendation from his friends Mer-

senne and Gassendi. Of one other friend and warm
admirer we know little. This was Du Verdus, a noble
of Languedoc. They had become so intimate that
Hobbes was about to give up all hopes of returning
to England, and to settle with Du Verdus in the
country, when a new career seemed to open for him
on the arrival of the Prince of Wales in Paris.

English refugees had been following the first fugi-
tive. The Cavendish family had taken the royalist
side. Hobbes's pupil, the third earl, had been im-
peached in 1642, and escaped to the continent. He
returned to England in 1645, submitted to the parliament, and lived in retirement at Latimers in Buckinghamshire till the Restoration. His younger brother,
Charles, had distinguished himself on the king's side
at Edgehill, but was killed in an encounter with
Cromwell in 1643. Their mother, Christiana, remained
in England, and her house was a meeting-place of
the royalist party, by whom she was fully trusted.
Their cousin, the Earl of Newcastle, commanded the
king's forces in the north, and when his army, then
led by Prince Rupert, was crushed at Marston Moor,
he left England and reached Paris in the spring of
1645. He stayed there three years, and his presence
was, no doubt, important to Hobbes. His wife repeats
a conversation between them, at which Newcastle
spoke sceptically of witchcraft, and, according to
her, suggested a passage to the same effect in the
Leviathan. Possibly the lady was claiming a little too
much for her husband. Bramhall, Bishop of Derry,
had escaped with Newcastle, and had a discussion with
Hobbes about free will at the house of the marquis
(as he had now become). Each of the disputants

afterwards put his arguments in writing; but Hobbes desired that his paper should be kept private. He had allowed a copy to be taken for a friend, which was afterwards published without his consent, with results to be presently noticed. Edmund Waller told Aubrey that he had met Hobbes, Gassendi, and Descartes dining together at the marquis's table in Paris. With the marquis at this time was his brother, Sir Charles Cavendish, who had been prevented by deformity from bearing arms, and had taken to mathematics. He collected, says Aubrey, as many mathematical MSS. as filled a hogshead, intending to publish them. But he died "of the scurvy contracted by hard study," and his papers, falling into ignorant hands, were sold by weight to the pasteboard makers. Petty mentions Hobbes's kindness in introducing him to the two brothers. Petty, most versatile and ingenious of men, was thirty-five years younger than Hobbes. He was precocious from childhood, and at this juncture was in Paris with an introduction to Hobbes from the English mathematician Pell. Petty helped Hobbes by drawing figures for his optical propositions; and the two joined in reading Vesalius's anatomy. Petty was soon afterwards lecturing on anatomy at Oxford. The economic writings by which he is remembered show marked traces of Hobbes's political influence. About this time, 1646, Clarendon, writing at Jersey on his way to Holland, sent a message to Hobbes asking for the *De Cive*, and told him that their common friend, Sidney Godolphin, slain at Chagford in the beginning of 1645, had left him a bequest of £200. Hobbes received £100, with a promise of the rest from

Godolphin's brother, to whom, though personally
unknown, he dedicated the *Leviathan* in gratitude.
At the end of the book he makes a striking reference
to his friend. "I have known clearness of judgment
and largeness of fancy, strength of reason and grace-
ful elocution, a courage for the war and a fear for the
laws and all eminently in one man ; and that was my
most noble and honoured friend, Mr. Sidney Godolphin, who, hating no man, nor hated of any, was
unfortunately slain in the beginning of the late civil
war, in the public quarrel, by an undiscerned and
undiscerning hand." The bequest must have been
welcome. It was not so easy to make communications
or send remittances, and Hobbes only heard of his
legacy by the accident of Clarendon's letter, some
little time after Godolphin's death. The Cavendishes
had plenty of calls upon their money, and had other
things to think of than Hobbes's fortunes.

The gathering of the exiles at Paris naturally led
to Hobbes's appointment to be mathematical tutor to
the Prince of Wales. It was, we may suppose, not a
very splendid post if regarded from a pecuniary point
of view. Newcastle had been for a time the prince's
'governor," and had drawn up a paper of instructions,
superfluously advising that the boy should not be too
devout, "and should be very civil to women." He
might now naturally recommend his friend Hobbes,
whose qualifications were indeed ample. Mersenne
had published some of his scientific speculations.
Pell had at this time confuted one Longomontanus,
who claimed to have squared the circle ; and Hobbes
was invited along with Descartes and other leading
mathematicians, including Sir Charles Cavendish, to

pronounce an opinion upon the controversy. How far he succeeded in impressing the prince with his reverence for Euclid does not appear. At a later time the conjunction was regarded as fraught with disastrous consequences. Burnet scented a diabolical plot. The Duke of Buckingham, such was the suggestion, desired to corrupt Charles's morals and principles. Buckingham would be in no need of help in the moral department, but he introduced Hobbes to inculcate "political and religious schemes," which made a deep impression upon the pupil, "so that the main blame of the King's ill principles and bad morals, was owing to the Duke of Buckingham." As a matter of fact, Hobbes states in a letter to Sorbière that he was confined to mathematical teaching, the prince being too young for philosophy. It would be more plausible to attribute to his influence Charles's most creditable peculiarity—a certain interest in science. Ill principles were abundant enough in the atmosphere of the court. The connection lasted at most for two years, as Charles came to Paris in 1646, and left it for Holland in the spring of 1648. He retained, however, a friendly feeling for his tutor. The new edition of the *De Cive* was now on the point of publication, and Sorbière, in 1647, proposed to describe Hobbes on the title-page as tutor to the Prince of Wales. Hobbes objected in a remarkable letter. The connection of the writer may do harm to the prince, as suggesting that he approves Hobbes's principles. Courtiers may accuse him of vanity. Finally he may think of returning to England if peace is established in any way. He did not, he said, belong to the household, and apparently found it already uncongenial.

Hobbes's teachership was interrupted, if not terminated, by a severe illness which brought him to the point of death in 1647. He gives a characteristic anecdote in regard to it. Mersenne was called in by a common friend, who feared that Hobbes would die outside of the Roman communion. Mersenne accordingly came and began a discourse upon the power of his church to remit sins. "Father," said Hobbes, "I have long gone over that question in my own mind. You have something pleasanter to say. When did you see Gassendi?" Mersenne dropped the subject. Soon afterwards Cosin, afterwards Bishop of Durham, offered his services, and Hobbes received the sacrament from him according to the Anglican rite : a great proof, he observes, of his reverence for the episcopal discipline. Aubrey gives a very different version of the story. When divines came to him in this illness, he said, "Let me alone, or else I will detect all your cheats from Aaron to yourselves." But Hobbes's own account must be preferred. Mersenne died in September 1648, after great suffering under the hands of blundering surgeons. Hobbes continued to work at his political writings. In 1650 he published or allowed the publication of the little treatise which had remained for ten years in manuscript, and in 1651 he published an English translation of the *De Cive*. The poet Waller had offered to translate it before, but having asked Hobbes to translate part by way of model, declined to undertake a task which, as he sensibly judged, could be executed by no one so well as the author himself. These two books were forerunners of the *Leviathan*, which was printed in London, and appeared in the middle of 1651. In August

Hobbes had another illness, of which the shrewd and learned physician, Gui Patin, gives a lively account. He was called in to see Hobbes, whom he describes as stoical, melancholy, and *outre cela Anglais*. Naturally, therefore, he had been thinking of suicide; Englishmen have a turn that way. He refused to be bled: the remedy for almost all diseases according to Patin. Next day, however, he gave in, to his great benefit. They at once became *camarades et grands amis*; and Patin allowed him to drink as much small beer as he liked. Hobbes was in the habit of saying that he would prefer an old woman who had been at many bed-sides to the "learnedst young unpractised physitian." The fate of his friend Mersenne may have weakened his faith in the faculty. Two months after his re-covery Charles reached Paris after his final defeat at Worcester, and Hobbes speedily presented him with a manuscript copy of the *Leviathan*, "engrossed in vellum in a marvellous fair hand." It is now to be seen in the British Museum.

The immediate consequence was that Hobbes had to retreat to England, and became the object of accusations which require notice, not because they are plausible but because they illustrate his position at the time. Wallis, in a controversy with Hobbes after the Restoration, declared that the *Leviathan* was "writ in defence of Oliver's title." Claren-don reports that he talked with Hobbes shortly before the book was published. Hobbes showed him some sheets and spoke of his opinions. Clarendon asked how he could publish such doctrine? After a "discourse between jest and earnest," Hobbes replied: "The truth is I have a mind to go home." Conver-

sations between jest and earnest reported twenty
years later are unsatisfactory evidence, and it is more
likely that the grave Clarendon failed to see a joke
than that Hobbes meant to make such a confession.
To Wallis he made a sufficient answer. Cromwell
did not become protector till 1653, and it could
not be known in 1650 that he was the right person
to flatter. But besides this the argument of the
Leviathan was certainly not modified in order to
please either Cromwell or the Rump, to which for
the present he was subordinate. The principles are
identical with those of the early treatise and the
De Cive written long before; and since they were
not modified at all, they were not modified in order
to curry favour with anybody. Things, it is true,
had changed, and it might be suggested that the
defence of the absolute power of the sovereign was
applicable to parliament, when it became sovereign,
as it had once been applicable to the king. But
parliament would certainly not admit that only by
success were its claims justified, or approve of a
doctrine which condemned the whole rebellion. In
any case it is scarcely fair to blame Hobbes, who
laid down a perfectly consistent doctrine from first
to last, if a change of circumstances made the doctrine
agreeable to a new order. The truth is, I take it,
that his view was one which could not be openly
avowed even by Cromwellians or by royalists. The
more they might act in accordance with it, the more
anxious they would be to disavow it.

There was, however, one part of the *Leviathan*
which might be a stumbling-block. In a *Review
and Conclusion* he briefly considered the question,

at what time does a subject become obliged to a conqueror? He answers that "it is when the means of his life are within the guards and garrisons of the enemy." Submission, therefore, to a *de facto* government is right; and Hobbes adds that such submission is not even an assistance to the new power, which would otherwise confiscate an opponent's whole property instead of taking a part. This was a convenient argument. In 1656 Hobbes could take credit for the influence of the *Leviathan* in framing "the minds of a thousand gentlemen to a conscientious obedience to the present government [Cromwell's], which otherwise would have wavered in that point." In 1662 he looks at the question from the other point of view, and remembers that by "compounding" they diminished the plunder of the usurper, and in due time would be better able to serve the king. That was the case of many honourable persons, including it may be observed, Hobbes's own patron the Earl of Devonshire. No moralist, I suppose, would deny that such submission becomes right in time. Nobody could blame an elderly scholar, who had no position under the exiled king, for settling down quietly in his native country and justifying the same action in his friend's case. No doubt, however, the doctrine gave offence to those who held out. "Mr. Hobbes," writes Sir Edward Nicholas in February 1652, 'is at London much caressed as one that hath by his writings justified the reasonableness and righteousness of their arms and actions." Hobbes had certainly not done that; but the royalist might be scandalised when an eminent writer, who had previously been the king's tutor, defended submission to the powers in existence, and so far admitted the cause to be hopeless. How far he was "caressed" does not appear. He certainly got nothing from the government, and he had very sufficient reasons for leaving France.

Nicholas was then in Holland, and previous notes of his are significant. "All honest men here," he says in January, "are very glad that the K. hath at length banished from his court that father of atheists, Mr. Hobbes, who, it is said, hath rendered all the queen's court, and very many of the D. of York's family atheists, and if he had been suffered, would have done his best to have likewise poisoned the king's court." A very few days later he regrets that Papists "(to the shame of the true Protestants) were the chief cause that that grand atheist was sent away." He mentions, but declines to believe, a report that the Marquis of Ormonde was very slow in signifying the king's command to Hobbes to forbear coming to court. Clarendon, who seems to have had some part in the expulsion, had now read the printed book and told Hobbes that "such a book would be punished in any country in Europe." He says that Hobbes had to "fly secretly, the justices having endeavoured to apprehend him." Hobbes himself says that the Anglican prelates had found fault with the theology of his book, and that he was in fear of the Catholic clergy, whose church he had certainly attacked. Whether Hobbes could rightly be called an atheist is a question to be noticed hereafter. His friend Mersenne had declared some years before that there were some 50,000 atheists in Paris alone, and that twelve might be often found in one

house. As there was no religious census at the time
the numbers must be considered as distinctly con-
jectural. "Atheism," however, is a word which could
be and was used simply as a missile to be hurled at
anybody morally or philosophically objectionable.
Both Hobbes's friends, Gassendi and Mersenne, were
Catholic ecclesiastics who discharged their functions
regularly, and Gassendi maintained that his admiration for Epicurus was consistent with thorough
orthodoxy. Hobbes can hardly have talked atheism
to them, and the anecdote about Mersenne and Bishop
Cosin, to which he refers so complacently, seems to
imply that he was as reticent as might be expected
from his timidity. Perhaps he had been more out-
spoken among the courtiers, and, at any rate, the
attacks upon the spiritual power in his two last
books meant an attitude towards the Church which
might well suggest "atheism," as Mersenne understood the word, even to candid critics. Certainly
he had said enough to shock the Catholic authorities, and his fear of their action was natural. Besides
this, he tells us that he was frightened by the murder
of the two English envoys in Holland and Spain,
Dorislaus and Ascham. He was in an awkward
position. Charles, he admits, was set against him.
The young king "trusted in those in whom his
father had trusted," says Hobbes. Hobbes was
hardly called upon to stay in a place where his
countrymen and the native authorities agreed in
considering him to be an atheist, and held atheism
to be not only damnable but criminal.

He was glad to escape to England in a severe
winter, and suffering from his infirmities, and to

settle among old friends in a land where he was at least permitted to publish his writings. Three months later (as he declared) he went more than a mile to take the sacrament according to the Anglican rite. He made his submission to the Council of State and remained for the rest of his life in England. In 1653 he again became a member of the Earl of Devonshire's family. The earl, though living in retirement at Latimers in Buckinghamshire, also occupied "Little Salisbury House" in London. Hobbes complained that, although the earl had a good library and provided his old tutor with all the books he wanted, a country life gave small opportunities for "learned conversation." One's understanding, Aubrey said, as Johnson might have said, "grows mouldy." He appears to have spent most of his time in London, and, as at all periods of his life, cultivated the friendship of his most distinguished contemporaries. He was on intimate terms with the best known poets, Waller, Cowley, and Davenant. Milton would not be a congenial friend. In his last year at Paris he had been very intimate with Davenant, who was then writing the first cantos of his ponderous epic *Gondibert*. He submitted it as it was written to Hobbes, and addressed a very long preface to his friendly critic. Hobbes replied in a letter which was printed as an appendix to the preface. It is superfluous to say that each expresses a very high opinion of the other's merits. I need not dwell upon Hobbes's æsthetic doctrine. "A poet," he says, "ought to know well, and to know much": a sign of the first is "perspicuity, propriety, and decency"; a sign of the second is "novelty of expression, which pleaseth by excitation of the mind, for novelty causeth admiration and admiration curiosity, which is a delightful appetite of knowledge." He ends by a spirited protest against Davenant's depreciation of old age as second childhood. "That saying, meant only of the weakness of the body, was wrested to the weakness of mind by froward children, weary of the controlment of their parents, masters, and other admonitors." The dotage of age is "never the effect of time but sometimes of the excesses of youth." "Those who pass their youth in making provision only for their ease and sensual delight are children still at what years soever: as they that coming into a populous city, never going out of their inn, are strangers still, how long soever they have been there." There is, moreover, "no reason for any man to think himself wiser to-day than yesterday, which does not equally convince he shall be wiser to-morrow than to-day." Davenant will love to change his opinion when he becomes old, and "meanwhile you discredit all I have said before in your commendation because I am old already." Hobbes was not quite sixty-two when he wrote this and was to live nearly thirty years longer. He did his best to act up to his encouraging but rather questionable doctrine, and took the approach of old age with all possible gallantry. Old age was then considered to begin at a comparatively early period, and Hobbes, in spite of the antagonism which he excited, enjoyed some of its privileges. Cowley's ode to him written some years later touches the point:

> " Nor can the snow which now cold age does shed,
>   Upon thy reverend head

> Quench or allay the noble fires within,
> But all which thou hast been
> And all that youth can be thou 'rt yet,
> So fully still dost thou
> Enjoy the manhood and the bloom of wit
> And all the natural heat but not the fever too."

A phenomenon which is accounted for in the familiar
lines :

> " To things immortal time can do no wrong,
> And that which never is to die for ever must be young."

Cowley says that the scholastic philosophy, of which,
as his poems show he had made some study, was now
dead, and that Hobbes is the great "Columbus of
the golden land of new philosophies." Hobbes's three
poetical friends had probably all known him in France.
Waller had an unfortunate facility for turning his coat,
and came back about the same time as Hobbes; he
was pardoned and then patronised by Cromwell, and
afterwards reconciled himself to Charles II. Davenant
finished his *Gondibert* in the Tower, but was afterwards allowed to revive theatrical performances before
the Restoration. Cowley, who had been trusted in
confidential employment by Henrietta Maria, was
suspected, like Hobbes, of a disposition to reconcile
himself to the actual authorities, but seems to have
been a consistent royalist.

Hobbes had two other remarkable friends. One was
Harvey (1578-1657) whose great discovery of the
circulation of the blood had been first published in
1616, and of whom Hobbes always speaks with profound admiration. Harvey is said to have left him
£10 in his will.[1] The other was John Selden (1584-

[1] Aubrey reports that Selden, like Harvey, left £10 to his
friend, but this seems to be an error.

1654). Their acquaintance began by Hobbes sending him a copy of the *Leviathan*, after which, says Aubrey, there was a strict friendship between them. The conversations between the authors of the *Leviathan* and the *Table Talk* would no doubt be worth hearing, and Selden's Erastian views would be thoroughly acceptable to Hobbes. Baxter, however, reports on the authority of Sir Matthew Hale, that Selden attacked Hobbes's sceptical opinions so forcibly as to drive him out of the room. Another of Aubrey's stories is that Hobbes dissuaded Selden from sending for a clergyman when he was dying. "What," he is supposed to have said, "will you that have wrote like a man now die like a woman?" As a contradictory account is given of Selden's death, and as Hobbes certainly acted on the opposite principle when he was himself in danger, we may probably assume that the anecdote represents not what actually happened, but what somebody thought would naturally be done by an "atheist."

Meanwhile Hobbes was, as he says, in a country where every one might write what he pleased. Free from fear of priests and with some gratitude to sectaries, he could sit down to finish his philosophy. He had sufficiently expounded his political theories, and they were provoking some controversy. Filmer (best known from Locke's attack upon his posthumous book, the *Patriarcha*) criticised Hobbes in 1652, along with Grotius and Milton. Alexander Ross, whose memory is preserved only by a rhyme in Hudibras as to the "philosopher who had read Alexander Ross over," animadverted on the *Leviathan* next year. But they were opponents who might be neglected by a writer who had now achieved so high a position.

Hobbes sat down to finish his work by completing
the exposition of first principles, from which he had
been distracted by his interest in the parliamentary
struggle.

He was presently interrupted. The anonymous
person to whom he had entrusted a copy of his discussion with Bramhall was now induced to publish
the piece in which, as he said in a preface, the author
of the *Leviathan* had solved a question over which
divines had wrangled so long and so fruitlessly.
Bramhall naturally supposed that Hobbes, who had
stipulated at the time for privacy, was responsible for
the publication. He therefore published all that had
passed with his rejoinder to Hobbes. Hobbes replied
in 1658, and Bramhall two years afterwards came out
with *Castigation of Mr. Hobbes's Animadversions*, together
with an appendix called *The Catching of Leviathan the
Great Whale*. This was meant to expose the atheistical
doctrine embodied in Hobbes's chief work. Bramhall
died in 1663, and Hobbes, who declares that he had not
heard of the attack for ten years, now made a reply
which did not appear till after his own death. The
controversy brought out some of Hobbes's most vigorous
writing, and gives an important part of his philosophy,
of which I shall have to speak hereafter. Hobbes
meanwhile had finished the book which was to give the
foundations of his system. It was published in Latin
as *De Corpore* in 1655. An English translation (only
superintended by himself) appeared in 1656.

This book contains a very important exposition of
Hobbes's general principles. It also includes certain
very unfortunate speculations which led to one of the
most singular tangles of controversy in which a philo-

sopher ever wasted his energies. I have already noted Hobbes's condemnation of the universities, which had found sufficient expression in the *Leviathan.* According to him, they still taught nothing but the old scholasticism, corrupted youth by classical republicanism, and were ignorant of modern science. He was not aware, it seems, of the remarkable change which had come over his own university. In 1619 Sir Henry Savile had founded professorships of geometry and astronomy. Until that time, according to Hobbes, many people regarded geometry as "art diabolical," and its professors, as Wood says, were taken to be "limbs of the devil." Mathematical studies were now gaining respect, and by the time of Hobbes's return to England, Oxford had become the meeting-place of a remarkable number of eminent and energetic teachers. Never before—perhaps one might add, not often afterwards—was the university so important a focus of scientific illumination. Oxford (alternately with London) was the headquarters of the remarkable group of men who founded the Royal Society after the Restoration. Young men destined to become famous, Robert Boyle and Christopher Wren and Hobbes's friend, Petty, and others less generally known, were of the number. Boyle, the eldest of the three, was thirty-nine years and Wren forty-four years younger than Hobbes. They represented the new generation, eager to enter into that promised land of science of which Bacon had caught "a Pisgah sight." The two Savilian professors, both some years older, were men of mark. Seth Ward (1617-1689) had been appointed professor of astronomy in 1649, though previously ejected from Cambridge for refusing the covenant. He was already known as an able mathematician, though after the Restoration he left science to rise in the Church and become ultimately Bishop of Salisbury. John Wallis (1618-1703), the professor of geometry from 1649, was a man of singular acuteness, and one of the first mathematicians of his day. His *Arithmetica Infinitorum*, published in 1655, was the greatest step towards the development of the differential calculus, elaborated by Newton and Leibnitz in the next generation. Oxford while represented by such men could certainly not be condemned as behind the time in science. Hobbes, who specially claimed to represent the scientific movement, should have recognised the men who were its most efficient organs. Unluckily for him things fell out very differently. Ward replied to Hobbes in an appendix to a book mainly directed against another assailant of the universities.[1] In an earlier essay he had professed a high opinion of that "worthy gentleman," Hobbes; but he now felt bound to expose the worthy gentleman's arrogance and ignorance. Backed by a letter from the famous John Wilkins, at this time warden of Wadham, and afterwards the first secretary of the Royal Society, he accused Hobbes of plagiarism, and taunted him in advance. Whenever Hobbes published his geometrical discoveries (of which he had apparently been boasting) he would find that they were only too well understood at Oxford.

These discoveries saw the light in the *De Corpore*. Hobbes had squared the circle: and though the sub-

---

[1] John Webster, known also from his *Displaying of Supposed Witchcraft* (1677), directed against Henry More and other credulous persons : and not the famous dramatist, as others have had to prove.

ject was strictly irrelevant, he could not refrain from
introducing a chapter into his book by way of showing
his capacity. He had solved the problem which had
baffled all previous geometers from Archimedes down-
ward. No man ever made a more unlucky boast.
Ward and Wallis agreed to make an example of the
rash intruder who had given himself into their hands.
Ward wrote against the general philosophy ; in that
department nothing could be done beyond repeating
familiar arguments. Wallis, who undertook the
mathematics, had a more satisfactory task. Mathematical controversies have the peculiarity that they
lead to definite issues, in which one side must be
entirely in the right, and the other entirely in the
wrong. Hobbes had or had not squared the circle, and
his success or failure could be clearly demonstrated to
all competent people. As a matter of fact, of course, he
had failed egregiously. Not only so, but he had made
successive attempts ; falling out of one blunder into
another, he had left traces of the process by cancelling
sheets, and he had shown a strange incapacity for even
appreciating the conditions of strict mathematical
proof. All this Wallis explained in an *Elenchus
Geometriæ Hobbianæ*, adding reproof and ridicule to
poison the wound to his victim's vanity. Hobbes was
too incompetent even to know that he had been refuted.
With a courage worthy of a better cause he defended
his own errors, and gave fresh proofs of incapacity by
attacking Wallis's real discoveries in *Six Lessons* for the
Oxford professors. Wallis in return gave *Due Correction for Mr. Hobbes in School Discipline for not saying his
Lessons right*. The language became worse, and diverged
into irrelevant topics. Wallis charged Hobbes with

confusing the Greek words Στιγμή and Στίγμα.
Hobbes's next book was therefore headed " Στιγμαὶ
'Αγεωμετρίας, 'Αγροικίας, 'Αντιπολιτείας, 'Αμαθείας or
*Marks of the absurd Geometry, Rural Language, Scottish
Church Politics, and Barbarisms of John Wallis.*"

When the Royal Society was founded, 1662, Hobbes
was naturally not invited to join a body of which his
antagonists were leading members. He showed his
anger by attacking Boyle's account of his experiment
with the air-pump. He often said that if people who
tried such a farrago of experiments were to be called
philosophers, the title might be bestowed upon apothe-
caries and gardeners and the like. Besides stating that
the Society was on the wrong tack and would learn
nothing till they adopted his principles, he indulged in
a personal fling at Wallis. Wallis replied in the
Hobbius Heauton Timoroumenos, which seems to have
been the most complete exposure of Hobbes's manifold
blunders. It gave Hobbes, however, his one telling
retort. Wallis made the accusation of disloyalty already
noticed. Hobbes defended himself, and pointed out
that Wallis had deciphered the king's despatches taken
after Naseby, and had boasted of the fact. If Wallis
now said (as he seems to have done) that he did it to
the king's advantage, that would only show that he
cheated his employer, excused treason with treachery,
and was a double spy. To this awkward thrust Wallis
did not reply. But it did not prove that Hobbes had
squared the circle.

The battle was not yet ended. Four years later
(1666) Hobbes came out with a new treatise, in which
he admitted that all geometers were against him;
either he alone must be mad or he alone not mad;

unless indeed they were all mad together. He was now
seventy-eight, but still wrote treatises to which Wallis
punctually replied until 1672, when Hobbes was
eighty-four. Wallis then dropped off, but Hobbes
published yet another treatise in 1674, and fired a
final shot called the *Decameron Physiologicum* in 1678,
at the ripe age of ninety.[1]

There is something pathetic as well as comical in
this singular history. Hobbes told Sorbière in 1656
that he attacked the professors mainly because they
represented the clergy and universities. That was a
very bad reason for assaulting his opponents' strongest
side. The old gentleman certainly wasted a great
deal of time and temper, and showed an amazing
degree of self-confidence. Still he was near seventy
when the fight began, and to a man of that age something should be forgiven for intellectual energy, even
in a mistaken cause. One remark may, I suppose, be
made. A man who attempted circle-squaring at a
later period proved himself to be hopelessly at sea.
Many such adventurers are described in De Morgan's
very amusing *Budget of Paradoxes*. But in Hobbes's
day the enterprise was not so clearly perceived to
be hopeless. He was called in, as we have seen, to

---

[1] A full account of this controversy is given in Croom
Robertson's *Hobbes*, pp. 167-185. I have been content to
follow him, and have not even seen Wallis's pamphlets which
have become rare, as he declined to print them in his works
after Hobbes's death. Robertson was far more competent than
I could be to give an opinion upon the merits of a controversy
which in any case would not deserve any lengthy discussion in
the present book. Dr. Tönnies thinks Robertson rather hard
upon Hobbes, and unjust to the historical significance of this
controversy.

arbitrate in one case of circle-squaring, and his friend
Mersenne had a controversy about the same time with
the Jesuit, St. Vincent, "the best of circle-squarers."
To square the circle, or in other words to find the
ratio of the radius to the circumference, was of course
a rational problem, though, I suppose, that the proper
treatment could not be applied till the development of
the methods adopted by Wallis, and so unfortunately
misunderstood by Hobbes. He persistently protested
against the application of algebra to geometry : that is,
against the most essential step in advance that was
being made in his day. He consequently made an
attempt in which failure was inevitable. De Morgan,
however, seems to feel a certain compunction in
classing him with the circle-squarers, and says, that
in spite of his blunders he shows great ability in his
remarks upon the general theory of mathematical
reasoning.

The moral is, I suppose, that a man ought to read
Euclid before he is forty. He will assimilate the
principles better, and he will also be made aware of
the danger of mistaking blunders for original discoveries. That is an error of which he will be cured
by examiners. Anyhow, besides wasting his energy,
Hobbes had put himself in a curiously uncomfortable
position by the time of the Restoration. Intellectual
audacity combines awkwardly with personal timidity.
The poor old gentleman, aged seventy-two, whose
great aim was to keep out of harm's way, had stirred
up an amazing mass of antipathies. His political
absolutism was hateful to constitutionalists like
Clarendon as well as to the more popular politicians :
to the two parties, that is, which were about to become

tories and whigs. Anglican bishops and non-con-
formist divines agreed that he was an atheist, and,
what was to some almost as bad, a hater of all ecclesiastical authority. His political views might suit the
courtiers, but no one could be more hostile to their
leanings to Rome. Political absolutism and religious
scepticism made a creed which could not be openly
avowed, though it might and did excite some tacit
sympathy. He had, however, spoken with a certain
authority as a representative of science. Now the
scientific and philosophical world had ostracised him.
They had pronounced him to be a charlatan. A man
who could make such a mess of squaring the circle was
presumably a paradox-monger in philosophy. His
opponents would taunt him with a failure admitted by
every one but himself. It is true that popular opinion
looks upon philosophers with a dash of amused contempt. Like Shakespeare's fools they are allowed a
certain license. Their queer opinions, even if atrocious, are so far removed from practical business as to
be harmless and rather amusing playthings. Personally Hobbes was generally agreeable; and so venerable
in appearance that one would prefer to leave him in
quiet. He had some anxious moments, but on the
whole was tolerated.

Hobbes had spent the winter of 1659 in Derbyshire, when Aubrey wrote to beg him to be present
at the king's arrival in London. Hobbes was
standing at the gates of Little Salisbury House
as his majesty's coach drove through the Strand.
Charles recognised his old tutor, took off his
hat and greeted him kindly. A week afterwards
Hobbes attended when Charles was sitting for his

portrait to the famous miniature painter, Samuel
Cooper, and diverted the sitter by his "pleasant discourse." Charles gave orders that he should always
have access to the court—the royal taste was good in
the matter of "wit and sharp repartees." When
Hobbes appeared, the king would say : " Here comes
the bear to be baited"; and the courtiers did their
best. Hobbes feared none of them, being "marvellous
happy and ready in his replies." He took care, however, to avoid serious topics. During the following
period, Hobbes spent most of his time in London.
Our next glimpse of him is given by the French
ambassador, the Comte de Cominges. Louis XIV. had
at this time resolved to become the patron of learned
men throughout Europe. Cominges was directed to
inquire what men worthy of this exalted patronage
were to be found in England. He made the dis-
couraging reply that arts and sciences had chosen
France as their sole abode. In England men still
remembered Bacon, Sir Thomas More, and Buchanan,
but the only living author of reputation was "*un
nommé Miltonius*" : an infamous person whose writings
would not be to the taste of the great king. Shortly
afterwards he discovered Hobbes, and invited him to
dinner along with the famous mathematician, Christian
Huygens, and Hobbes's old friend Sorbière. The
"*bonhomme*" Hobbes speaks enthusiastically of Louis,
and he might truly be called "*assertor regum*" (a title
which "*Miltonius*" clearly did not deserve) and
Cominges would be very glad to be the means of
obtaining a pension for him. Never, he says, "will
any favour have been better placed." The application
was favourably received at first, but nothing seems to

have come of it. Perhaps on inquiry somebody
remembered that Hobbes had left France in bad odour
with the priests, to say the least; or Huygens, upon
whom a pension was bestowed, may have given a
confidential opinion about the squaring of the circle.
Hobbes's friends anyhow denied at his death some
report of a designed or actual pension. Charles, however, had given him a pension of £100 a year. An
undated petition shows that it had been stopped for
some time along with others; but Hobbes says he
had enjoyed it to his great comfort for many years.
He mentions arrears in his will (1677). Sorbière next
year wrote an account of his travels with due compliment to Hobbes. The third earl, he says, "loves and
reveres" his old tutor. He applies Charles's saying
about baiting the bear to the clergy; and adds: "I
know not how it comes to pass, the clergy are afraid
of him."

Hobbes was certainly afraid of the clergy. The
years 1665 and 1666 were marked by the plague and
the fire of London, which naturally startled contemporaries. The fire of London might perhaps be set down
to the Papists, as was recorded on the monument, but
they could hardly have been responsible for the plague.
That was doubtless a manifestation of Divine wrath;
and to the question, what had provoked it? the
obvious answer was, Hobbes. A bill was brought into
parliament for the suppression of atheism and pro-
faneness, and a committee was instructed to receive
information about "Mr. Hobbes's *Leviathan.*" With
him was joined an eccentric Catholic priest, Thomas
White (or Albius), known at the time as a contro-
versialist. White was suspected of heresy. He had,

it seems, denied the "natural" immortality of the soul. Hobbes and White were doubtless not the only offenders. The court was not perfectly pure. The bill passed the House of Commons but was ultimately dropped. Hobbes was frightened, and not without reason. Aubrey mentions a report (probably referring to this time) that some of the bishops made a motion "to have the good old gentleman burnt for a heretie." Hereupon, he says, Hobbes put some of his papers in the fire. Hobbes wrote an essay concerning heresy to prove that he could not be legally burnt, and protested in an appendix to a Latin translation of the *Leviathan*. The essay was not published, and Hobbes probably depended for safety less upon his logic than upon the favour of Charles and of Arlington. Arlington, the secretary of state, was a concealed Catholic. There were plenty of "Hobbists" at the court at this time, as Clarendon and Burnet sorrowfully confess. Arlington possibly preferred them to the Anglican bishops who were more dangerous enemies of his church. Hobbes, at any rate, addresses Arlington as the special protector of his old age. The first result was that Hobbes was not attacked but forbidden to give further utterance to his views. Charles forbade the publication of the *Behemoth*, written in 1668; and Pepys wishing to buy the *Leviathan*, "which is now mightily called for" (3rd September, 1668), found that he had to pay twenty-four shillings for a second-hand copy; whereas it had theretofore been sold for eight shillings. It is now, he adds, sold for thirty shillings. The bishops would not allow it to be reprinted.

A year later, one Scargill, a fellow of Corpus College, Cambridge, having maintained some theses in which phrases from the *Leviathan* were twisted to an offensive meaning, was expelled from the university, and induced to make a public recantation. He had gloried in being a Hobbist and atheist, and attributed his moral ruin to Hobbes's principles. After this alarm, says Kennett, Hobbes went more regularly to the earl's chapel, though he would not go to the parish church. He did not care for sermons. They could teach him nothing but what he knew. His fame meanwhile was spreading abroad. In 1669 he was visited several times by the Grand Duke of Tuscany, who took away a portrait and works of the philosopher, to be preserved among the most precious jewels of the Medicean library.

In 1668 Hobbes reached his eightieth year, and might have had other motives for silence than prohibitions by authority. He preserved his intellectual activity, however, almost to the last. Besides the books mentioned, he had, about 1659, according to Aubrey, and about his eightieth year according to his own account, written a Latin poem of more than two thousand elegiacs, versifying the *Historia Universalis* of Cluverius, and describing once more the usurpations of the spiritual power. In 1664 Aubrey begged him to write about law, when he answered that he could not count upon life enough. Few men could become law students at seventy-six. Aubrey, however, sent him Bacon's *Elements of the Common Laws*; whereupon he set to work, and produced a *Dialogue between a Philosopher and a Student of the Common Laws of England*. His especial aim was to confute Coke, as the worshipper of precedent. The dialogue was not finished; but it is noticed by Maine as showing that Hobbes had anticipated many of the legal reforms afterwards advocated by Bentham. A few years later he retired from controversy—not to silence, but to a new literary employment. In 1673 he published the *Voyage of Ulysses* : a translation into English quatrains of Books IX.-XII. of the *Odyssey*. This, it seems, was by way of experiment; and a year later he produced a complete translation both of the *Iliad* and the *Odyssey*. Nobody has yet, I believe, discovered that the work is a worthy rival of Chapman or Pope : a task which might perhaps have charms for some literary revivalists. The severest critic might be touched to silence at any rate by Hobbes's own apology : "Why did I write it ? Because I had nothing else to do. Why publish it ? Because I thought it might take off my adversaries from showing their folly upon my more serious writings, and set them upon my verses to show their wisdom. But why without annotation ? Because I had no hope to do it better than it is already done by Mr. Ogilby." It was at least a creditable occupation for a man of eighty-six. I will content myself with quoting the passage, which has often been quoted to prove that Hobbes could deviate into a really poetical phrase. It is from the famous meeting of Hector and Andromache :

> ' Now Hector met her with their little boy
>   That in the nurse's arms was carried,
>   And like a star upon her bosom lay
>   His beautiful and shining golden head."

In 1675 Hobbes left London finally, to pass the last four years of his life at Chatsworth and Hardwick. He was still at work ; his last scientific paper appeared

when he was ninety, and on the 18th of August 1679
he tells his publisher that he is writing somewhat to
print in English. In October he was attacked by a
complaint incurable at his age. "I shall be glad," he
said upon learning it, "to find a hole to creep out of
the world at." At the end of November the family
moved from Chatsworth to Hardwick, and Hobbes
declining to be left behind, was put upon a feather-bed
in the coach. The journey was too much for his
strength; an attack of paralysis soon followed, and he
died on December 4th. He was buried at the parish
church of Hault Hucknall. The family and neighbours who attended were "very handsomely entertained with wine, burnt and raw, cakes, biscuits, etc.,"
and a slab of black marble was placed upon his
grave. In the inscription he is called "*Vir probus et
fama eruditionis domi forisque bene cognitus.*" He had
amused himself it is said, by allowing his friends to
prepare epitaphs, and the design which pleased him
most, was a gravestone inscribed: "This is the true
Philosopher's Stone."

Hobbes left nearly £1000, "which" says Aubrey,
"considering his charity, was more than I expected."
He had given a piece of land to a nephew, and paid off
a mortgage of £200 with which the nephew had
encumbered his estate. Aubrey collects a few bits of
information, with provoking gaps, as to his appearance
and manners. This is a tantalising statement for
phrenologists: "His head was . . . inches in com-
pass (I have the measure) and of a mallet form
(approved by the physiologers)." He was unhealthy
in youth, but grew strong when about forty, and had
a fresh ruddy complexion. He had an ample forehead,

and "yellowish-reddish whiskers, which naturally turned up, a sign of a brisk wit." He shaved close, except a little tip under his lip—"though nature would have afforded a venerable beard," he abandoned that ornament, to avoid affectation of philosophic dignity. "He had a good eye, hazel coloured, which would shine when he became eager, as though there were a bright live-coal within it." Various portraits, one at the National Portrait Gallery, and two in the rooms of the Royal Society,[1] show a head which is marked both by acuteness and singular dignity of expression. Hobbes might have sat for a portrait of Plato, and is, I think, the best-looking philosopher known to me.

The following account of his habits refers presumably to his last years. He rose about seven, and breakfasted on bread and butter, then he walked and meditated till ten, he dined at eleven, as his stomach could not bear waiting till the earl's dinner at two. After dinner he took a pipe of tobacco and a nap, and in the afternoon wrote down his morning's thoughts. He had been much addicted to music in his youth, and practised on the bass viol. He had always books of "prick-song" lying on his table, such as Lawes's songs, and at night when he was in bed, and the doors made fast, so that he was sure of being unheard, he would sing aloud for his health's sake. He denied the common report, that he was afraid to be alone on account of ghosts. He was not afraid of spirits, but of being knocked on the head for five or ten pounds. Hobbes was evidently careful about his health, and a believer in bodily exercise. He played tennis " twice or thrice

[1] A photograph from one of the last is prefixed to Robertson's monograph.

a year" according to Aubrey—once a week says
Sorbière—when he was well over seventy. He illustrates more than one argument in the *Leviathan* by
reference to the game. In the country, where there
was no tennis-court, he walked up and down hill
till he was in a great sweat and then had himself
rubbed down. "'Tis not consistent with an harmonical
soul," as Aubrey observes, "to be a woman-hater,
neither had he an abhorrescence to good wine."
Kennett speaks of a natural daughter, whom he called
his *delictum juventutis*, and for whom he provided. But
if he had been habitually immoral, his respectable
opponents would hardly have refrained, as they in fact
did, from any accusation of the kind. He calculated that he had been drunk one hundred times in the
course of his life : which, says Aubrey, "considering
his great age, did not amount to once a year." The
arithmetic is erroneous ; but twice a year would hardly
bring him up to the average of his time. He could
never endure habitual excess, as Aubrey testifies, and
after sixty he drank no wine. He had some more
attacks of illness (a dangerous one in 1668) besides
those mentioned before, and his hand began to shake
about 1650. About 1665 his writing became illegible.

Hobbes had few books in his chamber; but
"Homer and Virgil were commonly on his table ;
sometimes Xenophon or some probable history, and
Greek Testament or so"—which seems to be a pretty
good selection. "He was wont to say, that if he had
read as much as other men, he should have known no
more than other men." He appreciated, that is, the
truth that it is more important to assimilate than to
accumulate materials of thought. Descartes, like

Hobbes, insisted upon, and exaggerated his ignorance of previous authors. He had read nothing, as Voltaire put it, *pas même l'Évangile.* The attitude was natural in men who were deliberately rejecting the established doctrines of their time, and trying to substitute a new scheme of thought built upon entirely new foundations. The man, as Robertson remarks, who began his career by translating Thucydides, and ended it by translating Homer, cannot be taken as a simple contemner of literature.

Aubrey was properly anxious to collect some of his hero's good sayings. If he did not succeed in making a long list, his fate was that which befalls most such enterprises. He should, like Boswell or like Hobbes himself, have carried a note-book in his pocket. One characteristic saying may be quoted. "He was," says Aubrey, "very charitable to those that were true objects of his bounty. He gave sixpence one day to a poor beggar in the Strand. Whereupon a divine asked him : "Would you have done this if it had not been Christ's command ?" "Yea," said he. "Why ?" quoth the other. "Because," said he, "I was in pain to consider the miserable condition of the old man, and now my alms, giving him some relief, doth also ease me." This shows perhaps that his practice was better than his ethical theory.[1]

[1] Hobbes received £50 a year from his patron besides occasional presents, such as £40 for the dedication of the *De Corpore.* He speaks (in the life) of his indifference to gain. No avaricious man, he declares, ever achieved a noble work. He had lived to study, and he condemns those who study for the sake of gain. His boast seems to be fully justified. His life was worthy of a philosopher, in spite of trifling foibles, due to temper or timidity. It is to the credit of the British

Before considering his theories, however, something may be said of the view taken of him by his contemporaries. I do not speak at present of the more serious antagonists who wrote upon his philosophy. It is enough to say here that they attacked him with remarkable unanimity. His predecessor, Bacon, was cited on all sides as a venerable authority. His successor, Locke, was adopted as a leader by the great majority of the younger thinkers. Hobbes impressed English thought almost entirely by rousing opposition. Possibly his opponents had more or less to modify their own position in order to meet his arguments; but to them at least it seemed that Hobbism was the upas tree to be cut down root and branch. The *Auctarium* gives a long list of contemporary writers upon Hobbes; but can only mention a solitary work done in his defence, and that anonymous. He was the typical atheist. "Atheism," no doubt, was a name bestowed upon a phase of sentiment common enough at the court of Charles II., as it had been, according to Mersenne, in Paris. The religious controversies of the Reformation period had naturally led to a "sceptical spirit," such as found utterance in Montaigne's immortal essays. The endless war of dogmas revealed the folly of dogmatism. Montaigne, though disclaiming philosophical pretensions, suggested philosophical problems to great thinkers like Pascal; but he was acceptable to less serious minds. The so-called

aristocracy of those days—who do not generally get many compliments—that one of them gave to the hated sceptic a support which made him virtually independent enough to devote his powers to philosophy, while he deserved it by honourable service.

"libertins," it seems, would alternately attack and
humble themselves before the priests, as they objected
to any moral police, or thought that, after all, absolu-
tion might be convenient. They could profess scepticism under cover of more serious thinkers, and then
make edifying ends to clear their scores. Probably
that was true of many Hobbists. Eachard, best known
by his book on the causes of the contempt of the clergy,
wrote in 1672 two very smart dialogues in ridicule of
Hobbes. He divides the followers of Hobbes into pit,
box, and gallery. The pit was filled by the sturdy
sinners who welcomed him as an ally against morality
in general; the gallery by fine gentlemen anxious to
show their wit; and the boxes by men of gravity and
reputation whose approval was more cautious. The
"Hobbist" was generally taken to be the shallow
infidel, who still figures in edifying tracts. The
character of the "town-gallant" (1680) says that "he
swears that the *Leviathan* may supply all the lost
leaves of Solomon, though, for anything that he has
read himself, it may be a treatise on catching sprats."
He has only learnt through the rattle of coffee-houses;
but the book maintains that there are no angels except
those in petticoats! A tract of 1686 describes the
"town-fop" as equipped with three or four wild companions, "half-a-dozen bottles of Burgundy, and two
leaves of *Leviathan*." In Farquhar's *Constant Couple*
(1700), the hypocrite pulls out of his pocket a book
supposed by his friends to be full of "pious ejacula-
tions," while he remarks to himself : "This Hobbes is
an excellent fellow." The only concrete instance of
such a Hobbist mentioned is Charles Blount (1654-
1693), the unfortunate deist, who killed himself because

he was not allowed to marry his deceased wife's sister. He published various tracts, including a sheet of sayings from Hobbes's works, and a tract borrowed from Milton's *Areopagitica*, and deserved to be regarded as something more than a "town-fop." According to Aubrey, Dryden greatly admired Hobbes, and in his plays made use of some of Hobbes's doctrines. I am not aware of any coincidence in confirmation of this. Dryden says himself that he was sceptical by nature, and before his conversion he may have sympathised with Hobbes's hatred of priestcraft; but his poems on religion do not seem to imply any familiarity with the *Leviathan*. Hobbes ceases about the end of the century to be the butt of all orthodox controversialists. In the following generation, Toland and Collins, who professed to be applying Locke's philosophy in the interests of free-thinking, became the regular objects for attacks, and Hobbes passes out of notice. Warburton, who loved acute paradox, notices the change, and speaks of Hobbes with a certain admiration; but he shared the fate of all his contemporaries, as the eighteenth century came to think the seventeenth hopelessly old-fashioned.

CHAPTER II

1. *Hobbes's starting-point and aims*

I REMARKED, superfluously perhaps, that the circumstances revealed by Hobbes's biography had an important bearing upon an appreciation of his philosophy. The two incidents to which he gives a place in his own life, the sudden revelation of the charms of Euclid when he was forty, and the conversation upon the nature of sense-perception, mark the impression made upon him by movements in the contemporary world of scientific and philosophic thought. On the other side, his position in the family of a great noble encouraged a keen interest in the controversies which distracted the political world. His own intellectual and moral idiosyncrasies of course determined his special attitude towards the great issues involved in both cases. Hobbes's idiosyncrasies are sufficiently obvious. He was, in the first place, a born logician. He loved reasoning for its own sake. His great aim was to be absolutely clear, orderly, and systematic. He desired,

---

[1] The *De Corpore*, which is the chief authority for the following chapter, is in the first volume of the Latin works in Molesworth's edition. An English translation superintended, but not written, by Hobbes, and containing some curious mistakes, forms the first volume of the English works.

in modern phrase, to effect the thorough unification of knowledge. Euclid fascinated him as constituting a complete chain of demonstrable propositions, each indissolubly linked to its predecessor, and every one confirming and confirmed by the others. A complete theory of things in general should, he thought, be a philosophical Euclid; and he hoped to lay down its fundamental principles and its main outlines. He shrank from no convictions to which his logic appeared to lead him; and he expounded them with a sublime self-confidence, tempered, indeed, by his decided unwillingness to become a martyr. Of course, like most men in whom the logical faculty is predominant, he was splendidly one-sided. When things seemed clear to him, he could not even understand that any difficulties existed for any one. That difficulties did in fact exist is plain enough to his readers, if only from the curious devices by which he is sometimes driven to meet them. But though to others he may appear to be evading the point, or adopting inconsistent solutions, to himself he always seems to be following the straightforward path of inexorable logic.

One-sidedness is a most valuable quality. It means willingness to try intellectual experiments thoroughly. A man who sees the objections to an hypothesis, is tempted not to give it a fair trial; the man who sees no objections, is tempted to force all doctrine into his own preconceived framework; but, on the other hand, he is more likely to bring into relief whatever truth it may really contain. He may at times show that what seemed to be merely paradox is an important element of the whole truth. More frequently, no doubt, he may enable others to perceive the precise

points at which his system breaks down. One-sidedness, it need hardly be said, implies defects. Hobbes,
for example, was not a poet; he had no sympathy for
the imaginative and emotional thinkers; he would
have been the last man to lose himself, like his contemporary, Sir Thomas Browne, in an *O Altitudo*, or to
soar into the regions in which the mystic is at home.
For him those regions were simply the habitat of
absurd chimeras, to be exorcised by downright hard-
hitting dialectics. He loved to be in broad daylight,
to base himself on the tangible facts which undoubtedly
must be recognised in a satisfactory system. Mystery
for him means nonsense, and is to be excluded from
all speculation whether upon geometry or religion.
Invaluable services are rendered by the active application of such an intellect; but clearly its possessor
is likely to say a good many things which will shock
people of a different turn, and his want of sympathy
with their sentiments may lead him to dismiss con-
temptuously and abruptly opinions which may conceal
important truth under vague imagery.

I must endeavour to set forth Hobbes's main positions
impartially, without attempting to go far into problems
which since his day have been discussed by generations
of philosophers, and which, I fancy, are not as yet
quite settled.

One point may be noticed at starting. Hobbes
gave his views of both "natural" and "civil" philosophy, to use his own terms. He has been criticised
both as a natural and as a civil philosopher, and
the one or the other part of his work has been made
most prominent according to the special purpose
or personal taste of the critic. This suggests the

inquiry, whether his interest in physical science or in
the nature of men and institutions gave the real starting-point of his speculation   A decisive answer can
scarcely be given, and an answer is of the less importance because his most characteristic point is precisely
his conviction that the two inquiries are inseparably
connected.   Hobbes appears to have been the first
writer who clearly announced that "civil philosophy"
must be based upon "natural philosophy," or,
in other words, that a sound "sociology" must be
based upon scientific knowledge.   He may be called
a Herbert Spencer of the seventeenth century, and
in spite of very wide differences, there is a certain
resemblance between the two thinkers.   Each of them
aims at exhibiting a complete system in which the
results of the physical sciences will be co-ordinated with
ethical and political theory.   Hobbes's attempt was of
necessity premature ; the essential data were not in
existence.   Physical science was still in its infancy ;
and Hobbes's own scientific knowledge was necessarily
as crude as that of his contemporaries, and had special
defects of its own.   The political philosophy, again,
however acute, was stated in terms of speculations
which have long become obsolete.   The *Leviathan*,
once so terrible, may be taken for an intellectual fossil
—a collection of erroneous assumptions and sophistries
which are confuted in a paragraph or two of the
students' text-books.   Perhaps our descendants may
be equally dissatisfied with systems which bulk very
largely in our eyes, though we may hope that they
will make allowance for our inevitable ignorance.

  If, however, thinkers did not break ground by framing "premature" schemes of doctrine, they would

never advance to riper and more durable schemes.
Great thinkers at least do something to test the solidity
of the old structures, and here and there lay a founda-
tion-stone or two, which will be built into the more
comprehensive edifices of the future. We are not
ourselves so far advanced in the social sciences that we
can afford to judge our predecessors with the confidence of men who have reached a definitive system.
The tentative gropings of a great man, trying to secure
a starting-point, are always instructive, and Hobbes
may at least show us what were some of the besetting
fallacies at an early stage of speculation. He certainly
has such merits in a high degree, though, as I think,
more decidedly in " civil " than in " natural " philosophy.

Hobbes succeeded in working out a legal or political
theory, which had a very genuine and powerful effect
upon the course of speculation. Few people accepted
the political doctrine generally attributed to him, and
most people repudiated it with indignation. Still it
influenced men, if only by repulsion, while much of
his argument has been adopted by others, and occasionally reappears in curiously different combinations. I
consider this to be the most important aspect of
"Hobbism." It may be said, too, that whatever was
his real starting-point—whether he began with political
opinions and then tried to bring them into connection
with his scientific views, or followed the reverse process—it was certainly the political doctrine which he
expounded most thoroughly and consistently. His
teaching, whatever its faults, has evidently been traced
out carefully and patiently, and is a complete elaboration of certain leading principles.

It is, however, essential to consider his views of

"natural philosophy." He contributed nothing to
the special sciences. His expositions of first principles
show inconsistencies which suggest that he had not
considered them with the sustained attention which
he devoted to his political writing. Nor does it appear
that he had so important an influence upon succeeding
schools of thought in this as in the other direction.
But he at any rate laid down in a most unflinching
and vigorous fashion certain doctrines which, to say
the least, startled his contemporaries, and so far must
have done them good. Theologians and moralists
paid him the compliment of taking him for their
most serious opponent. He was regarded as the
type, though almost a solitary instance, of inter-
necine hostility to established beliefs. Upon him,
we may say, were concentrated the various antipathies which in the nineteenth century were provoked by evolutionism, agnosticism, materialism, and
destructive criticism. That is to say, he personified
the tendencies of thought which are supposed to
result from the study, or the too exclusive study, of
the physical sciences. I express no opinion as to
the merits of the question involved. Everybody
admits that the physical sciences embody a vast
amount of definitively established truth, and that, so
far as they are true, they cannot be inconsistent with
any other truths. The problem is whether the alleged
incompatibility between the conclusions of legitimate
science and those of the accepted theology is really
insuperable, or only appears to be insuperable when
the man of science reads a false interpretation into
his doctrines.

Now Hobbes, according to the judgment of con-

temporaries, interpreted the scientific principles of
his day in a sense which made them totally irrecon-
cilable with orthodox belief, and anticipated with
great penetration some inferences which in later
years have shocked and alarmed believers. How far
Hobbes himself admitted or denied this will appear
presently. In any case he represents the first definite
emergence in English thought of an antagonism which
in later generations was to develop and to acquire an
absorbing interest. The scientific impulse of the time
had found its English prophet in Bacon. Whatever
his failure in the attempt to lay down the true
scientific method, his surpassing literary power enabled him to make a most imposing forecast of the
coming empire of man over nature. The men who
founded the Royal Society could appeal to Bacon's
vast reputation as sanctioning their enterprise. Now
they could do so without incurring any suspicion as
to their orthodoxy. Boyle, for example, one of the
chief leaders, was as conspicuous for his piety as for
his scientific zeal. There was nothing objectionable
in the precepts which direct a careful and methodical
study of phenomena in order to discover their laws.
"Baconian induction" implied no conception either of
the heterodox or of the orthodox variety. It rather
suggested that we should attend to facts and leave
ultimate principles to take care of themselves. Bacon
denounced the old scholastic subtleties which had
shown their futility in dealing with the physical sciences,
and by so doing he might in some degree discredit the
dogmatic system of theology associated with the old
philosophy. That, however, so it seemed to the more
liberal thinkers of the time, did not imply an attack on

natural theology, but rather the need of disengaging its truth from the scholastic logomachies by which it had been overlaid. The ablest English divines of the next generation sympathised with that doctrine.

In Hobbes the spirit of science first becomes dogmatic and aggressive. He lays down with the utmost calmness and confidence the most startling principles. He thinks them so reasonable and obvious that you might expect even a bishop to accept them. They are demonstrated once for all. The point of view from which he started is indicated by his two significant anecdotes. The scientific method which impresses him is that of which Euclid gave him the typical instance. It is a deductive method, which develops all its conclusions from undeniable first principles. He scorns the accumulation of experiments. The difficulty which impresses him, is not that we have not sufficient data, but that we do not reason upon them with rigorous accuracy. In the second place, the one universal phenomenon is motion. We see things changing their positions relatively to each other, and in the last analysis, that is really all that we can know or measure. Contemporary developments of science have impressed these convictions upon him. His view of them is sufficiently indicated in the "Epistle Dedicatory" to the *De Corpore*. He is struck by the novelty of science. The ancients, indeed, had done much in geometry, and left in it "a most perfect pattern" of their logic. Astronomy only began when Copernicus revived an ancient opinion which had been "strangled by a snare of words." Copernicus led to Galileo, whose discovery was the "first that opened to us the gate of natural knowledge universal, which

is the knowledge of the nature of motion." The
"science of man's body" was first discovered with
"admirable sagacity" by Harvey—"the only man I
know that, conquering envy, has established a new
doctrine in his lifetime." Extraordinary advances
have been made by Kepler and by Hobbes's "two
friends, Gassendi and Mersenne," to whom he would
have no doubt added Descartes, had Descartes been
equally friendly. "Civil philosophy is much younger,
as being no older (I say it provoked, and that my
detractors may know how little they have wrought
upon me) than my own book *De Cive.*" "There
walked in old Greece, indeed, a certain phantasm
for superficial gravity, though full within of fraud
and filth, a little like philosophy;" this was adopted
by the first doctors of the Church, who thus "be-
trayed the citadel of Christianity." Into it there
entered a theory called school divinity, walking on
one foot firmly, which is the Holy Scripture, but
halting on the other rotten foot, which the Apostle
Paul called *vain* and might have called *pernicious
philosophy*; for it has raised an infinite number of
controversies in the Christian world concerning religion, and from these controversies, wars. It thus
resembles the Empusa of the comic poet, having one
brazen leg, and the other the leg of an ass. By
putting into a clear shape the "true method of
natural philosophy" he will drive away the metaphysical confusion, "not by skirmish, but by letting
in the light upon her." The "Empusa" is to be
exorcised because she has strangled the infant science
by words. But what we have to do is not to follow
her through the monstrous labyrinth of sophistry

which she has spun over the world, but simply to
use our eyes and to look at the plain facts.

We have raised a dust, as Berkeley said afterwards,
and complained that we cannot see. Philosophy is now
among men, is the opening remark of the *De Corpore*, as
corn and wine were in the world in ancient time. There
were always vines and ears of corn; but as they were
not cared for, men had to live upon acorns. So every
man has natural reason; but for want of improving it,
most men have to be content with the acorns of "daily
experience." They show sounder judgment than those
who (like the schoolmen) "do nothing but dispute and
wrangle like men that are not well in their wits."
Hobbes proposes to "lay open the few and first elements of philosophy in general as so many seeds from
which pure and true philosophy may hereafter spring
up by little and little." He will show how to culti-
vate the corn and wine. Science, we have been told,
is nothing but organised common-sense. And Hobbes
anticipates this dictum.

Thus Hobbes's method is to be that which has
already borne fruit in the hands of the great thinkers
of the time. Geometry has already made a fresh
start. Copernicus has shown how the stars move.
Galileo will enable us to explain how each movement
is determined by previous movements. The science
of astronomy will thus be constituted by the help of
geometry. Then Harvey's great discovery suggests
that the human body also is a mechanism, the various
movements of which must be explicable on the same
principles. The circulation of the blood, like the
revolution of the planets, is simply a case of motion;
and when we have the facts and the laws of nature,

we shall be able to deduce all physiological phenomena, like all astronomical phenomena, by the help
of geometry. Hobbes assumes also that the same
methods will enable us to construct his "civil"
philosophy.

Meanwhile we see the general impression made
upon Hobbes by his studies in Euclid, and by his
doctrine that motion is the universal fact. It means,
in short, that he holds that the aim of all philosophy
is to give a mechanical theory of the universe. That,
again, is to say that he sees clearly what is in fact
the ultimate aim of all the physical sciences. The
scientific inquirer endeavours as far as possible to give
the rules embodied in all physical phenomena in terms
of time and space. He imagines a bewildering dance
of innumerable atoms, lying somehow behind the
visible world, moving in different directions, colliding,
combining and separating and going through the most
complicated evolutions. Perhaps the ignorant person,
or the profound metaphysician, may decline to believe
that there are any such things at all, or, at any rate,
to believe that they are the only realities. But even
if they do not exist, they have to be invented. Our
justification for creating them is that they enable us
to state the rules by which, from a given state of
things, we can accurately foretell the future or go
back to the past. They may be only a working
hypothesis, or may be realities which might con-
ceivably become visible or tangible. The method,
however, in any case, implies that the ultimate
problem is, as Hobbes said, one of geometry. The
atoms have no properties, except the property of
embodying certain laws of motion; and the whole

problem becomes that of stating how one state of
motion will pass into another. That is to say, it is
ultimately a problem of geometry or the measurement
of spaces. So far Hobbes agrees with Descartes:
"Give me space and movement, and I will make
the world." *Toute ma physique n'est autre chose que la
géométrie.* Hobbes undoubtedly was not so good a
geometer as Descartes; but they fully agree in principle. "They that study natural philosophy," says
Hobbes, "study in vain, except they begin at geometry; and such writers and disputers thereof as are
ignorant of geometry do but make their hearers and
readers lose their time." Civil philosophy must, as he
adds, be based upon physics, and therefore upon geometry. Both Hobbes and Descartes accepted Harvey's
discovery as giving a mechanical explanation of physiological phenomena. Descartes's doctrine that animals
are automatic was equally applicable to the working
of the human body, and Huxley has set forth with
his usual vigour and clearness the importance of this
doctrine in the development of physiology.

Upon such questions I can say nothing; and Hobbes
did not distinguish himself in that direction. But the
next peculiarity of his philosophy is marked by his
divergence from Descartes. In his objections to the
Meditations, Hobbes criticises the famous *"je pense:
donc je suis."* "I think" and "I am thinking," he
says, mean the same. Therefore the conclusion is
good: "If I think, I am." But it does not follow that
"I" who think am a spirit or a soul. On the contrary,
he declares, it would seem to follow that a thing which
thinks is something corporeal. I do not think that I
think, I simply think; or thought and its object are

one. Descartes complains that Hobbes has not
attended to a later passage in the *Meditations*, which
proves that the soul or thinking thing cannot be
corporeal. I need not go into the arguments. The
difference is indeed of that radical kind in which
argument rarely produces agreement. Descartes con-
ceives himself to have proved that the soul and the
body are of diametrically opposite natures, and though
he believes in both, thinks that our conviction of the
existence of the soul is more fundamental than our
conviction of the existence of the body. The complete
antithesis between the spiritual and the natural world
became of course a cardinal point of his system, and
generations of metaphysicians were to puzzle themselves over the nature of the intimate relation which,
as he also held, binds them in inseparable unity.

Hobbes, on the other hand, seems simply to ignore
this contrast. He takes for granted, for he scarcely
argues the question, that the material world is the
only world. In a later *Objection*, he gives it as his
own opinion that spirit is nothing but a movement
in certain parts of the organism. In other words,
thought, as well as every physical process, is a species
of the universal genus "motion." Hobbes is so far a
simple and thoroughgoing materialist. That of course
simplifies things. The whole of knowledge represents
for him an extension of the physical sciences. The
theory of the human body and the theory of the
political body are more complicated than the theory of
the stars; but we still have to do with nothing but
motion, though in forms more intricate and difficult to
measure. "The whole mass of things that are," he
says in the *Leviathan*, "is corporeal, that is to say,

body; and hath the dimensions of magnitude, namely, length, breadth, and depth; also every part of body is likewise body, and hath the like dimensions; and consequently every part of the universe is body, and that which is not body is no part of the universe; and because the universe is all, that which is no part of it is *nothing*, and consequently nowhere. Nor does it follow from hence," he adds, "that spirits are *nothing* : for they have dimensions and are therefore really bodies, though that name in common speech be given to such bodies only as are visible and palpable, that is, that have some degree of opacity." The last sentence is required by a consideration which frequently hampers his utterance. He is bound to admit that spirits exist, for spirits are mentioned in Scripture, and, for whatever reason, he will not contradict Scripture. But no proof can be given of existences of which it is impossible to have "natural evidence." All evidence appeals to the senses; but a spirit is taken to be that which does not "work upon the sense," and is therefore not "conceptible." When we use such words as "living, sensible, rational, hot, cold, moved, quiet," as he calmly remarks, the word "matter" or "body" is understood, all such "being names of matter." In "natural discourse," therefore, a "spirit" means a phantasm—a dream mistaken for a reality. The spirits mentioned in supernatural discourse must exist; they must therefore be bodies, for nothing exists except bodies; but they can be kept out of harm's way. As bodies they must be space-filling; but they are made of such subtle materials that they cannot act upon other bodies. They cannot make their existence known, for they cannot affect motion.

Motion is the cause of all things: "all mutation is
motion; motion can have no cause except motion";
and these flimsy entities are in the universe without
taking part in it. For us they are nonentities. If
motion can be caused by motion alone, that motion
can cause nothing but motion. Hobbes's opponents
inferred that, as thought is not motion, it must
have some other cause, or inhere in a subject which
is not material. Hobbes infers that as nothing
can exist which is not material, thought must itself
be motion.

This is really Hobbes's starting-point and guiding
principle. Man is an automaton; thought is a motion
in his brain; all his actions can be explained by the
laws of motion, like the motion of a clock or of the
Chatsworth waterworks. In the attempt to carry out
this conception thoroughly, Hobbes gets into various
difficulties. A modern materialist may perhaps urge
that the difficulties can be surmounted by a fuller
knowledge of physical science. The opposite explanation is that the initial assumption is radically false,
and that Hobbes's merit, as Professor Hoeffding says, is
that his consistent adoption of it brings out the
inevitable failure of a thoroughgoing materialism.

To understand him we must begin by granting his
postulate. Let us admit provisionally that man is
simply an automaton and yet that he can somehow
think, feel, reason, and become a philosopher.

First of all, however, Hobbes explains what is the
aim of his philosophy. Philosophy, according to him,
means a knowledge of the effects which will be produced
by given causes or, conversely, of the causes which have
produced given effects. We may trace the working of

the mechanism in order to make use of it for our own purposes. Philosophy then is strictly "practical" or "utilitarian," to use the common phrases. The "inward glory and triumph of mind" arising from our mastery of some abstruse question would not of itself repay the pains necessary to obtain the result. "The end of knowledge is power": a phrase which recalls Bacon's famous saying.[1] Both Bacon and Hobbes desire knowledge to enable men to rule the forces of nature. The utility of "natural philosophy" appears in such arts as navigation, architecture, and so forth; and we may see what they have done for mankind by comparing the civilised races of Europe with the Americans and "those that live near the poles." Since all men, as Hobbes assumes, have the same faculties, the whole difference is due to philosophy. "Moral and civil philosophy," however, is equally useful, though its utility must be measured not by the commodities which it gives but by the calamities which it obviates. The worst of calamities is war, especially civil war. From war proceed "slaughter, solitude, and the want of all things." All men know these to be evil. Why then do wars continue? Because men do not know the causes of war and peace. Few men, that is to say,

---

[1] "Knowledge is power," as Hamilton points out (Dugald Stewart's Works, v. 38) is a running title in the *Advancement of Learning* and may not be Bacon's own phrase. However, in the *Meditationes Sacrae* we may see in a theological context *ipsa scientia potestas est*: and this in the translation becomes "knowledge itself is power." See Bacon's Works, ed. Spedding, vii. 241, 253. It has often been denied that Bacon used the words, as in Bulwer's *My Novel*, where the wise confute a young man who has rashly adopted them. Anyhow, as Hamilton says, they clearly represent Bacon's meaning.

have learnt the "duties which unite and keep men in peace." Now " the knowledge of these duties is moral philosophy." Hobbes thus holds substantially a doctrine which was characteristic of a later period and was vigorously expounded by Buckle. The growth of civilisation means essentially the growth of knowledge. Knowledge will not only enable us to apply mechanical inventions, but will show the identity of human interests and lead to the extirpation of war. Hobbes's view of the methods by which this consummation was to be reached differed materially from that of the Utilitarians of the middle of the nineteenth century, but the general conception is the same.

He proceeds to define the "subject" of philosophy. It has nothing to do with theology (for pretty obvious reasons), nor with the doctrine of angels, nor of things (if such there be) which are not bodies, nor with revelation which does not appeal to reason, nor with astrology and other "divinations which are not well grounded"; nor with the doctrine of "God's worship," which is the "object of faith, not of knowledge." Moreover it excludes "history as well natural as political, though most useful (nay necessary) to philosophy"; for such knowledge is "but experience or authority, and not ratiocination." Philosophy deals exclusively with the "generation and properties" of the two chief kinds of bodies—the natural body, a work of nature, and the commonwealth, the body made by the agreement of men. "Civil philosophy," which deals with the last, is divisible into two: "ethics," which deals with human nature, and "politics," which deals with men as citizens. The treatise, therefore, which gives the general principles applicable to all philosophy is called *De Corpore*, since "body" includes all that is knowable.

2. *Logic*

The world is made of unchangeable but moving bodies. All that happens is the transformation of one set of motions into another according to certain fixed laws. Somehow or another we can ascertain these laws, and, when duly systematised, they become "philosophy," or a statement of necessary truths. What then is truth? Hobbes observes that "truth is not an affection of the thing, but of the proposition concerning it." The word "true" is often, but inaccurately, opposed to "feigned." But, properly speaking, if we say that a ghost or the image in a mirror is not a man, we do not assert that the ghost is "false," but that the proposition "a ghost is a man" is false. "A ghost is (still) a very ghost." Truth and falsehood belong to the reasoning process which is peculiar to man, upon whom it confers the privilege of framing "general rules." This privilege, indeed, is "allayed by another"; and that is by the privilege of absurdity, to which no living creature is subject but man only. And of men "those are of all most subject to it that profess philosophy." Nothing, as Cicero said, can be so absurd as not to be found in their books. Hobbes will explain the source of their errors.

Meanwhile we have a problem. Reality belongs to bodies; truth to propositions or thought. What then is that which thinks? Hobbes has replied that it is body, and thought is a movement in the body. But it is plain that if this be true, the thinking thing does

not directly perceive its own nature. Thought does
not present itself as a movement. We are not conscious of the physical processes which somehow constitute or underlie the thinking process. It follows
that as thoughts are not bodies, they are unreal—mere
nonentities or "phantasms," as Hobbes generally puts
it. Reality thus seems to be entirely divorced from
truth. The thought-process may be determined by
motion, but, as immediately known, it is a set of
imaginary phantasmagoria playing over the surface of
things but itself unreal. The "soul" is real in so
far as it is material; but the ideal world made of
phantasms is unreal. Yet somehow the soul manages
to reason by help of the phantasms, and to discover
the rules of bodily movement. The problem remains,
how this process is to be explained. Hobbes's answer
gives his theory of logic, and forms the first part of the
De Corpore. The title *Computatio sive Logica* indicates
his peculiar view. All ratiocination, he declares,
is computing. Reasoning is addition or subtraction.
Arithmeticians add or substract numbers; geometricians add lines and figures; logicians add names to
make affirmations; affirmations to make syllogisms;
and syllogisms to make demonstrations. The type of
reasoning for him is still Euclid. Adding and sub-
tracting suggest the process by which the square on
the hypothenuse in his favourite proposition may be
cut up and put together again so as to form the
squares on the two sides. He had a prejudice against
the new methods by which algebraic calculation was
being substituted for the direct intuitive methods of
geometry, and to the arithmetic which, in the hands
of the detestable Wallis and his like, was leading to

humbug about infinitesimals. Arithmetic, however, seems best to illustrate his view. Number, as he would say, is not "an affection of the thing." The same thing may be one or twelve, as we count in feet or inches. The unit is arbitrary. And yet numbering enables us to state the most essential properties of things. Ten or a hundred by itself is a mark of no particular body, and is therefore a nonentity. But it meant something very real that Hobbes's hundred a year came to just ten times ten pounds. Reasoning in general is counting with names or numbers. "Words," as he says, in one of his pithiest aphorisms, "are wise men's counters; they do but reckon with them, but they are the money of fools." The remark has a wide application; and, in this case, the "fools" are those who talk scholastic jargon. But it states his general principle. The "use of names in registering our thoughts," as he remarks elsewhere, "is in nothing so evident as in numbering." Once men could not count, except on their fingers, as is shown by the decimal notation. The names learnt in the right order enable us to perform all the operations of arithmetic.

Since the names are thus the counters, out of which we frame propositions, we have to ask, What is a name? Hobbes gives a famous definition. "A name is a word taken at pleasure, to serve for a mark which may raise in our mind a thought like to some thought we had before, and which being (disposed in speech and [1]) pronounced to others, may be a sign to them of what the speaker had or had not before in his mind." Names are thus "marks to ourselves." "How incon-

---

[1] Omitted by error in the English version.

stant and fading men's thoughts are, and how much
the recovery of them depends upon chance, there is
none but knows by infallible experience in himself!"
No man remembers numbers without the names of
numbers disposed in order and learnt by heart. The
name recalls not only the thing but the general rule.
The results given by reasoning without such helps
will presently slip from us. We should get on very
slowly if we had to find out the multiplication table
every time we did a sum. "Marks" are thus necessary to recall thoughts, and become "signs" when we
teach them to others, which is an essential condition
of the preservation and growth of science. To serve
as signs, again, it is necessary that names as marks
should be "disposed and ordered in speech." To
speak rationally, you must not only renew the memory
of a thing, but say what you are thinking of its relation to other things. For that purpose, again, words
may be useful which are not names of things, but only
of "fictions and phantasms of things." That words are
an essential instrument of thought which, without
them, could not, to say the least, get beyond rudi-
mentary and vague inferences is, I take it, a very
sound doctrine. Hobbes did good service by directing
attention emphatically to it. He managed, however,
to give it a strange twist. Signs, he remarks, may be
"natural" or "arbitrary." The cloud is a natural
sign of rain; a bush at a tavern door is an arbitrary
sign of wine to be sold. Now words are clearly
"arbitrary," as was signally proved in the Garden
of Eden, and again, at the Tower of Babel. This
is of course obvious. If "*homo*" meant in Latin
what "man" means in English, it is plain that the

sound employed as a mark varies "arbitrarily." But Hobbes sometimes speaks as if, because language is the instrument of reasoning, and yet uses arbitrary marks, reasoning gives arbitrary results. So, he says in his fourth objection to Descartes, reasoning may be simply an assemblage and concatenation of names by the word "is."[1] If that be so, he says, reason does not conclude to the nature of things, but only to their names; that is, it shows whether we are connecting them according to the conventions which we have made at fancy about their significations. Descartes naturally replies that we reason about things, not names; and that a Frenchman and a German may have the same thoughts though they express them in entirely different words. Three and two, says Hobbes elsewhere, make five, because men have agreed that "five" shall be the name of as many units as there are in three and two. That explains why we say "two" and "three" instead of "deux" and "trois," but does not prove that we can alter the truth expressed by arbitrary sounds. Definitions are "truths constituted arbitrarily by the inventors of speech, and therefore not to be demonstrated." We make such truths ourselves (*vera esse facimus nosmet ipsi*) by our consent to the use of names.

The doctrine, so stated, seems too absurd even for a philosopher (as Hobbes would have said), and certainly does not correspond to his own conviction of the infallibility of his demonstrations. It is inconsistent too

---

[1] He is careful to point out that the copula is not necessary, and that the meaning might be expressed by simply putting two names together. A mistake on this point leads to the invention of such scholastic terms as "entity."

with much that he says elsewhere. It seems to be a trick played upon him by his logic, for, trying to give a fall to his antagonists, he loses his own balance. His general line of thought is intelligible. Philosophy, we see, according to him, is formed by a chain of true propositions, linked or (as he puts it) added together. Each link is a syllogism; and reasoning demonstrates that, if the first propositions be true, all the dependent propositions must be equally true. Language is the essential instrument of the process, though language, as he admits, is not necessary to thought, only to the articulate thought which leads to science. We make inferences from "natural signs"; rain, for example, is suggested by clouds, though the inference is often erroneous, and no experience can be demonstrative. Again, a man though deaf and dumb may observe that the angles of a particular triangle are equal to two right angles; but only the man who has the use of speech can prove that the property is necessarily true of all triangles. "Experience concludeth nothing universally." It tells us that day and night have always followed each other; not that they always will follow.

Now, though "experience" suggests a kind of reasoning, it is only with the use of language that "ratiocination" properly begins. Science embodies "ratiocination." The validity of ratiocination depends entirely upon the correct use of its essential instrument, language. This, as Hobbes expresses it, means that the whole process is dependent upon definitions. If definitions were arbitrary, all science must be arbitrary. Nothing could be further from his mind than this conclusion, and what he really means may

be gathered from the purpose of his argument.
Philosophy aims first at deducing effects from causes.
Definitions are the "primary propositions" from
which this process starts. The definitions, therefore,
of "all things that are caused, must consist of such
names as express the cause or matter of generation."
When we have defined the circle as the figure made
by "the circumduction of a body whereof one end
remains unmoved," we can deduce all the properties
of the circle. Geometrical relations enable us to
determine the motions of the body, and therefore the
relations of cause and effect. Theories of motion, of
"physics," and ultimately of ethics and politics, are
founded upon geometry, and geometry itself follows
from the definitions. Euclid, it is true, lays down
certain axioms, but Hobbes argues that the axioms
themselves follow from the definitions. He deduces
the axiom, for example, that "a whole is greater than
any part thereof," from the definition of "greater."
Demonstration requires ratiocination, and ratiocination
is only possible when we start from definitions which
are "nothing but the explication of our simple conceptions." The "principles of ratiocination consist in
our own understanding, that is, in the legitimate use
of such words as we ourselves constitute." The
meaning seems to be that geometrical truths owe
their peculiar certainty to the fact that geometry is
through and through an intellectual construction.
We can understand it, because in some sense we make
it. The definitions, then, are not "arbitrary" in the
sense that any other combination of words would do
as well, or that the properties of a figure would alter
if we defined it differently. By "arbitrary" he means

rather "artificial," or somehow made by us and not
by the things. The words are mere counters, or
instruments for calculating which we devise for the
purpose. We make them as a workman makes keys
for opening locks. He may make what tools he
pleases, but it does not follow that they will serve his
purpose equally well. We make the key ourselves,
but all keys will not open the lock.

We may define a figure by any of the properties
peculiar to it; we may regard a circle as made by the
revolution of the radius or as the figure which will
enclose the maximum area by its circumference. But
we must somehow find the mode which will actually
generate it. The definition marks the point at which
we have got hold of the thing by its right end, or have
so organised our "simple conceptions" that they explain the "generation" of the more complex. The
mind must find the appropriate instruments, though
when Hobbes thinks of them as of simple creations out
of nothing, he uses "arbitrary" in an apparently absurd
sense. His theory thus becomes feasible, and suggests
a real answer to the problem as to the special prerogative of mathematical proof. How far it contains
truth is a question which I must leave to writers who
can walk confidently in the perplexing border region
between mathematics and metaphysics.[1]

[1] One remark may be made parenthetically. Dugald Stewart,
in a passage which had a great effect upon J. S. Mill (as Mill
tells us in his Autobiography), takes Hobbes's view of definitions
in geometry. Definitions serve generally to prevent ambiguity,
and in geometry they serve as the real principles of our reasoning. He then remarks that Condillac has said that propositions,
equations, and judgments are at bottom the same thing. This
he ridicules, observing that Condillac would be surprised to

To complete our sketch of his logical scheme we must glance at the process by which we get from the definitions to the demonstrated truths. Names are put together to form propositions and propositions to form syllogisms. Hobbes accepts the ordinary rules about syllogisms, of which he gives a brief summary. The question remains, What, according to him, is the ultimate nature of the process? Why is the syllogism demonstrative? Now, in the first place, as a thorough nominalist, he denies the existence of any "universals" except names. Man is the name of Peter, John, and so forth, but there is no such thing as an universal man. We have an "idea" of one man, for every idea is one and of one thing. There is no "idea" of man in general, and the mistake arises from supposing that what is true of the name is true of the idea. In "nature," that is, there are only individuals, not classes. Now in the syllogism we seem to learn something from referring the individual to a class. Since Peter is a man, he has the properties of a man. What, then, is the implied logic? Hobbes's answer is simple. A proposition is true "when the predicate is the name of everything of which the subject is the name." " Man is a living creature " is true, "because everything that is called man is also called living creature." The syllogism carries us a step further by "adding" an

find that he was reviving the "obsolete conceit" of an old English writer, i.e., Hobbes. Evidently, the *De Corpore* had fallen into oblivion in Britain, though in Stewart's time, if not in Condillac's, it was exciting great interest in France. Stewart himself, it would seem, had hardly got beyond the first chapter, or he certainly would have been candid enough to mention that he too was reviving a doctrine of the old writer.

affirmation. Take, for example, "every living creature
is a body; man is a living creature; therefore man
is a body." The minor premise is true, if the predicate "living creature" is a name of the same thing
as the subject (man). The major premise is true if
the predicate (body) is a name of the same thing as the
subject (living creature). Therefore "the three names
are also names of the one and the same thing," or
"man is a body" is a true proposition. He goes on to
explain what "passes in the mind" when we syllogise.
We "conceive the image of a man speaking" and
remember that "what so appears is called man"; we
have the image of the same man moving, and remember
that what so appears is called "living creature"; and
finally the image "filling space" is called "body."
Thus the three names are names of the same things.
Hobbes has told us before that the proposition "man is
a living creature" is true because it pleased man to
impose both these names on "one thing," and declares
that the truth is therefore "arbitrary."

This queer doctrine still entangles him. If we only
call a thing a "man" which we also call a "living
creature," the proposition "man is a living creature"
must be verbally true. We have agreed to put a mark
only where there is another mark. But that does not
explain why "man" applies to John, Thomas, and
Peter, not to a stick or a dog, nor what is meant by
calling these three men "living creatures." Hobbes's
account of what passes in the mind implies indeed that
the words are in some way defined. We call that
"man" which has the faculty of speech, and that
"living creature" which moves; and possibly by
remembering Hobbes's doctrine as to definitions we

may attribute to him a more rational meaning. He is always thinking of his Euclid. The definition of a circle tells us how it is generated, and enables us to deduce all its properties, or to infer that a figure which has one property has also the others. The different names describing the properties apply to the same thing, though the "thing" is not a mere simple unit but a complex of relations If then "man" and "living creature" are modifications of "body," and if we could tell how they are "generated" in conformity with certain laws of motion and of various combinations of matter, we could deduce all the properties of the species from simple definitions, and see how one attribute such as "speaking" was a product under certain conditions of "moving" or "living." The premises of the syllogism would express the relations between the various classes thus formed. The whole proceeding is for Hobbes "arbitrary," because the process is carried out in the world of "ideas" or "phantasms" which we make or organise for ourselves —for thoughts are not "things," but unreal entities, which, for some reasons that he has not explained, correspond in some way to the facts. Moreover, in the case of "syllogising," we come to a difficulty of which he will, as we shall see, try to find some solution. A phenomenon is presented to us in the concrete, and we do not know the underlying process by which it has been evolved out of the simpler elements. We cannot in the least say how faculty of speech is related to life in general. We can only say that, somehow or other, one thing or one name includes the other : and that appears to be an "arbitrary" assumption made to enable us to reason.

G

3. *Physical Science*

Whatever is the explanation of Hobbes's strange assumption that names must be "arbitrary" in order that reasoning may be demonstrative, we have the old difficulty. Certainty belongs to the world of thought; but thought is "unreal" and the words which are its tools can be put together at pleasure. Reality belongs to fact which is hidden behind the phantasms. How do we get across the chasm which divides them? What are the "things" which lie behind the veil of thoughts? This leads to a further speculation. Hobbes tells us that the things to which we give names are of four kinds : bodies, phantasms, "accidents" and names themselves. I need say nothing of the "accidents," an irrelevant intrusion which bothers him a good deal. The real distinction is between bodies and phantasms, and the question is how they are related.

Here we come to a remarkable result. Hobbes seems to be diverging from his thoroughgoing materialism. Geometry and the laws of motion will not be sufficient for the problems that meet him. Having expounded his logic, he comes in the second part of the *De Corpore* to the first grounds of philosophy. It is rather startling to find this rigid materialist declaring that time and space are, as we now say, "subjective." Descartes begins by doubting whether our sensations really prove the existence of an external world, and finds doubt insuperable. Hobbes begins by asking what would happen if we supposed the whole external world to be annihilated. He answers that it would make no difference. We should still have our "ideas of the world." They are mere "phantasms, happen-

ing internally to him that imagineth," but will still
appear to be "external" and independent of the mind.
Moreover, even if outside things are taken to remain,
"we still compute nothing but our own phantasms."
We mark out our measurements of the stars and the
earth "sitting still in our closets or in the dark."
Space is not an affection of the body. Otherwise, when
a body moved, it would carry its place away with it.
Time is equally a phantasm. A year is time, and yet
nobody thinks that a year is "the accident or affection
of any body." The past and future do not exist, and
consequently days, months, and years must be "the
names of computations made in our minds." He
therefore defines space as the "phantasm of a thing
existing without the mind simply," and time as "the
phantasm of before and after in motion." When space
and time are thus declared to be mere "phantasms,"
and therefore to have no existence outside of the mind,
and when, moreover, we are told that our reasoning
depends entirely upon them, we are well on the way to
Berkeley's idealism or Hume's scepticism. "Phantasms," or "ideas"—he uses both words,—are the ultimate elements of our thoughts; and it would be the
next step to declare with Berkeley the non-existence of
matter, while Hobbes already agrees with Hume that a
soul is a superfluity. With Hobbes, however, body, it
appears, is still the reality and the only reality. Space,
he has told us, is "imaginary because a mere phantasm,
yet that very thing which all men call so." Now suppose the thing previously annihilated to be created
over again. Then it must, in the first place, fill some
part of the imaginary space and, in the second place,
must have "no dependence upon our thought."

Hence he defines body to be " that which having no
dependence upon our thought is coincident or co-
extended with some part of space." A body, he tell us
afterwards, has "always the same magnitude, but does
not keep the same place." "Place is nothing out of
the mind, nor magnitude anything within it." "Place
is feigned extension, but magnitude true extension."
Place is immovable, whereas bodies move. It appears,
therefore, that there is real space by which the
magnitude of any body is measured, and space is imaginary. It must, so it seems, be both purely objective and purely subjective. Though the phantasm is
unreal, it somehow enables us to know the realities.

The peculiarity of Hobbes's position is just this :
that he does not perceive that any problem is
raised by the contrast between soul and body—the
world of thought and the world of things. He does
not seek for any hypothesis, such as Spinoza's
one substance with infinite attributes, intended to
bring the two worlds into unity. Bodies are still
independent of thought, and are the sole and
absolute realities. Thought is a mere play of phantasms, which are unreal because only in the mind.
Yet the phantasms give us knowledge of the bodies
which go on placidly moving outside of thought ; and
the mind, which knows only its phantasms, is aware
of the outside world, and is itself a set of motions in
that world. That, it seems, must be simply taken for
granted and no explanation is required. It never
suggests any scepticism as to the possibility of knowledge. Hobbes will be as dogmatic as if no difficulty
existed. Nobody, as is already sufficiently evident,
could be more profoundly impressed by that conception

of the universe which is indicated by such phrases as the "reign of law" and the "uniformity of nature." All phenomena without exception present themselves in conformity with certain general rules. The future could be absolutely foreseen and the past recalled if we had the required knowledge. From the existing state of the solar system, the astronomer could say what it was at any preceding, or what it will be at any succeeding epoch. These powers indeed are limited by the enormous complexity of the calculations and of the facts to which they are applied. Other sciences are less perfect because they have to deal with more intricate problems, but not because any science includes a really arbitrary element. From the minutest to the most universal phenomenon, everything that will happen is already predetermined. The fall of a leaf or the explosion of a world is equally part of the single unalterable system of things. Spinoza was to give the most impressive version of a theory which may be appalling to some minds, and simply self-evident to others; but Hobbes was not less possessed with the conviction than his greater follower.

This mode of interpreting the universe is implied by the theory of cause and effect which he now expounds. As we have sufficiently seen, "all mutation is motion," and the changes of motion are simply the modification of previous motions. Cause, he says, is the aggregate of all the accidents of the agent and the patient. Omitting his technical word "accident," we may say that whatever motion takes place in a thing is determined by the whole set of previous conditions. If all the conditions necessary for a given effect are present, it will "necessarily" happen; and if one of them be absent, it will necessarily not happen. Whatever happens has a "necessary cause," looking backwards, and looking forwards a necessary effect. "Causation and the production of effects," he adds, "consist in a certain continual progress." Causation, that is, is not with him a mere sequence of disconnected phenomena, but a continuous process, in which one set of motions is always being transformed into another. We may "in imagination" divide the process into two parts at any assumed instant; we shall then call the preceding part the cause, and the succeeding part the effect. The same causes will of course always produce the same effect, since they differ in nothing but time. The conception of power again suggests different ways of looking at the same process. The "power of the agent" is what is called the "efficient cause." We use the word "power" when we are thinking of the future, and "cause" when we are thinking of the effect as already produced. The power of the patient, again, is what is called the "material cause," with reference to the effect which will be produced by the "efficient cause," and both together are the entire cause. Besides these the traditional scheme recognised also "formal" and "final" causes. The "formal," according to Hobbes, are superfluous. "When it is said that the essence of a thing is the cause thereof, *as to be rational is the cause of man*, it is not intelligible; for it is all one as if it were said, *to be a man is the cause of man*, which is not well said." A "final cause," again, "has no place but in such things as have sense and will," and in that case, as he undertakes to prove, it is an "efficient cause."

The rejection of "final causes," Bacon's "barren

virgins," is inevitable. It is indeed obvious that the
conception is altogether out of place from Hobbes's
point of view; that is, from a thoroughgoing
mechanical explanation of the universe. What we
have to do is to trace the series of movements of the
whole set of interacting bodies. At every stage the
motion of each body is the resultant of its own previous movement and of the movement of the various
bodies which have come into contact with it. Why
does a projectile move in a certain direction and with
a certain velocity ? The answer is given by its previous state, and the explosive or restraining forces
which have modified that state. Each of these forces
means that other bodies have come into contact with
it and modified its conduct in accordance with the
laws of motion. So far, obviously, we have nothing
to do with "end" in the sense of purpose. We are
tracing a single process backwards and forwards. If,
again, we take a mechanism, such as the clock, which
plays so conspicuous a part in the illustration of "final
causes," we explain the movement of the hands by
the various wheels, chains, and so forth which transmit motion from the weight or spring. If we trace
the process backward, we come to the point at which
the clock itself was put together. The cause then
is the set of processes, including on the one hand the
muscular movements of the clockmaker, and on the
other, the movements impressed upon the materials.
All that man does is to move one bit of matter to or
from another. The clockmaker's actions, again, are
determined by his purpose, by his "end," and the
means which his calculations prescribe for securing the
end. But now, according to Hobbes, the clockmaker

is just as much an automaton as the clock. His per-
ceptions, calculations, and motives are movements in
his brain, due to the impact of external bodies upon
the organs of sense and the reaction which takes place
in the brain. They are the "efficient cause" of the
clock, and the so-called "final cause" is merely a name
for the same set of processes absolutely determined by
the preceding processes. The man desires and expects,
but the senses and expectations are themselves part of
the movements implied. It is clear that from Hobbes's
point of view, the so-called "final cause" is a mere
name for the efficient cause, considered in one relation,
and that the whole series of events is purely mechanical.
Hobbes, it is true, professes to believe in a Creator
who once put the world together and must have
intended whatever comes to pass; but science can only
trace the series of events and ask what was the preceding state from which any given state is generated.
The fact that everything was intended does not explain how everything comes to pass; and to diverge
from the question how things actually happen to the
question why they should happen is to leave the
ground of science and to get merely nugatory answers,
diverting us from the right line of real investigation.

One other point is characteristic of Hobbes's system.
Whatever happens, he holds, happens necessarily.
Moreover, whatever does not happen is impossible.
"Every act which is not impossible," as he puts it,
"shall at some time be produced." There is no
such thing as contingency. "That is called contin-
gent," he says, "of which the necessary cause is not yet
perceived." That is to say, it is not only "necessary"
that, if the solar system was put together in a certain

way, certain results should follow, or that if a sparrow
is shot, he should fall to the ground; but it is also
necessary that the solar system should be just what it
is, and that the sparrow and the shot should have
come into collision just when they actually did.

Omitting certain deviations into mathematical speculation and circle-squaring, we come in the last part of
the *De Corpore* to an important step towards the
solution of a difficulty already indicated. We have
now to consider "Physics or the phenomena of nature."
He gives theories of light, the tides, and gravitation,
and it is needless to say that upon such matters it
was impossible for him to reach any valuable results.
His view of the proper method of treatment, however,
implies an important doctrine. "Philosophy," as we
have seen, may either deduce effects from causes or
causes from effects. Hitherto he has confined himself
to the first—the deduction of effects from causes. He
has been able to start from definitions—from the
truths which we "create ourselves"—and he has, as
he maintains, affirmed nothing except the definitions
themselves, or the propositions which can be logically
inferred therefrom : that is to say, "nothing which
is not sufficiently demonstrated to all those that agree
with me in the use of words and appellations ; for whose
sake only I have written the same." But now we
have to change the method. We start from "the
appearances of nature," which are known to us by
sense. Our first principles are not such as are impressed by definitions, "but such as being placed in
the things themselves by the author of nature, are by
us observed in them ; and we make use of them in
simple and particular, not universal propositions."

The senses, as we have already seen, give only empirical knowledge, which is made up of merely probable statements, such as "clouds are a sign of rain," and cannot reveal those necessary truths of which alone science consists. This would be the point at which we might expect something about the Baconian methods of induction. Hobbes takes a different line.

We are to reason about phenomena : and "of all phenomena or appearances which are near us, the most admirable is apparition itself, τὸ φαίνεσθαι : namely, that some natural bodies have in themselves the patterns almost of all things, and others of none at all." By the patterns (*exemplaria*) he means the "phantasms" which exist only in the thinking bodies— in men, not in stones. What then is the cause of these "ideas and phantasms which are perpetually generated within us"? Since they are continually changing, they must be due to some change "in the sentient." Since all change is motion, again, this implies that the senses are due to motion in the organs of sense. The object is some "remote body," from which pressure is propagated to the organ, and the consequent endeavour or reaction of the organ. "Endeavour" he has defined in a previous passage to be "motion made in less time and space than can be given; or motion through the length of a point, and in an instant or point of time." Sense, then, is the phantasm made by the "endeavour" outward in the organ, which is reaction against the endeavour inwards from the object. Something very like this may be read in modern books, which tell us how the stimulus to the nerve transmits molecular movement to the brain, and sets up a reflex action. Hobbes, however, could only speak very vaguely, and

takes for granted much now exploded physiology. He
is a little doubtful about one point. Some philosophers
have maintained that "all bodies are endued with sense."
If sense were made by reaction alone, their argument
would be unanswerable. It is, however, the possession
of organs by living bodies which makes the difference.
The organs preserve the motions set up in them:
whereas in inanimate bodies the motion or reaction
must cease as soon as the external pressure ceases,
and the phantasm which it causes vanishes instantane-
ously. Sense, to be of any use in giving knowledge,
must be accompanied with memory, for the knowledge
which it gives depends upon the comparison of the
phantasms. This suggests one of his significant
phrases. "It is almost all one for a man to be always
sensible of one and the same thing, and not to be
sensible at all of any things," or, in his pithier Latin,
"*sentire semper idem et non sentire ad idem recidunt.*"
Imagination, again, is "nothing else but sense decaying or weakened by the absence of object." The
difficulty remains, how memory, which is thus necessary for the comparison of phantasms and all knowledge
derived from the senses, can be interpreted in terms
of motion. It seems as if we still required a mind
different from the organ to look on and compare the
decaying senses. Self-consciousness remains a mystery.
Hobbes answers Descartes's "*Je pense*" by saying
that we cannot have a thought of a thought; but he
holds that memory is a feeling of a feeling. *Sentire se
sentisse, meminisse est.*

This involves another remark. Hobbes insists emphatically that the phantasm is somehow quite different
from the motion by which it is caused. He had already

pointed out in the *Human Nature* that people easily
fancy that colour and shape belong to the object, or
that the sound is in the bell. The opinion has been
so long received that the contrary must seem a paradox. Yet the common view involves the introduction
of the old "species visible and intelligible": it is "worse
than a paradox—an impossibility." The colour and
"image" are "nothing without us." They are apparitions due to the motions in the brain.[1] The senses are
deceptive, as when men "divers times" see objects
double, or take a reflected image for a reality, or see
a flash of light from a blow on the eye. The same is
true of the other senses. Smells and tastes vary from
man to man. The heat which we feel from the fire is
manifestly in us and not in the fire, for it gives pleasure
and pain, "whereas in the coal there is no such thing."
The "paradox" is now a familiar truth. Hobbes
seems to go beyond his immediate successors. They
would admit that the so-called "secondary qualities,"
colour, and so forth, are purely subjective; but the
primary qualities, space and solidity, seemed to have
superior claim to "objective reality." Hobbes observes
that place and time, that is to say, magnitude and
duration, "are only our own fancies of a body simply
so called"; that is, of a body considered without reference to its other properties.

All our knowledge of phenomena depends upon the
senses, and what the senses present to us are simply
the unreal phantasms, upon which, it would seem, no

---

[1] In a dedicatory letter of an unprinted treatise upon optics,
he says that he had stated this theory to Newcastle about
1630; and appeals to him as a witness: the same doctrine
having been since published by another.

real science or body of demonstrable truths can be
erected. The cause of the phantasms, again, is the
"endeavour" of the organ—infinitesimal movements
which take place within the length of a point. Hobbes
here denies emphatically that "infinite" has any real
meaning beyond "indefinite," whether indefinitely
great or small. Men who profess to reason about the
infinite and eternal are "not idiots, but, which makes
the absurdity unpardonable, geometricians, and such
as take upon them to be judges." They get entangled
in words to which there is no corresponding idea, and
"are forced either to speak something absurd, or,
which they love worse, to hold their peace." No
limits, however, may be assigned to possible greatness
or smallness. Microscopes now show things a hundred
thousand times bigger than they appear to bare eyes,
and might be made so as to magnify each part a
hundred thousand times more. So we now know that
the distance from the earth to the sun is but as a point
in comparison with the distance from the sun to the
fixed stars. Hobbes was impressed by these recent
revelations of the enormous vistas opened by early
science, which have become still more impressive as
science has grown. They suggested to him the impossibility of building up scientific knowledge on the
direct basis of observation. Everything depends upon
motion; but the motions which are causes of the
phantasms or of natural phenomena are too infinitesimal
to be perceived. Their existence may be inferred, but
their precise nature can only be guessed. When,
therefore, we proceed, from the phenomena given by
sense, to the causes, we can no longer start from the
definitions which, in the previous inquiry, state our

first principles. We have instead of that method to start from hypotheses. Hobbes aims at showing some "ways and means by which they [appearances] may be, I do not say they are, generated." He ends his discussion of the phenomena by declaring that the hypotheses which he has assumed are "both possible and easy to be comprehended," and that he has reasoned rightly from them. "If any other man will demonstrate the same and greater things from other hypotheses, there will be greater praise and thanks due to him than I demand for myself, provided his hypotheses are conceivable." At any rate he has got rid of empty words, such as "substantial forms," "incorporeal substances," "antipathy," "sympathy," and "occult quality."

So far it seems that Hobbes's method was that of modern sciences. Their aim, like his, is to give a mathematical theory of the various natural forces, such as heat, light, and electricity. They begin by a hypothesis about atoms and molecules which must be conceivable, and represent such properties of matter as we know to exist, although no direct observations can reveal them. If, again, these assumptions enable us to formulate the observed "laws," and to predict what will happen in other cases, and if no other assumptions can satisfy the conditions, we regard the successful assumptions as proved, or at least as provisionally established, though, it may be, in need of modification or of some further assumptions which may make them more complete. The difference is that the vast improvement both in instruments of observation and in methods of mathematical calculation enable us to apply incomparably more searching

tests to our hypotheses, as well as to gain confidence
from the reciprocal support given to each other by
different departments of investigation. Hobbes had
to be vague and audacious, and make erroneous physical assumptions. He was still in the period of Descartes's vortices, and could not anticipate Newton's
theory of gravitation.

His physical speculations have therefore no interest,
except as specimens of the early guessing with which
men had to be content at the dawn of science. The
general conception of the possibility of working out
mathematical theories of physical sciences shows that
he was fully awake to the most important movement
of thought in his own day, and ready, in spite of his
odd misconceptions, to adopt the results of the great
teachers, such as Galileo and Harvey. But we have
now to look at another point. The "motions" or
"endeavours" in the bodily organs which generate
the phantasms of the senses, generate also, as he
remarks, "another kind of sense . . . namely, the
sense of pleasure and pain," which he fancies to proceed from the action of the heart. This doctrine he
takes to be favoured by Harvey's discovery. It is
clear, however, that here we come to a difficulty.
What we know directly are the phantasms : the sensations of light, heat, and so forth, or the pleasures and
pains which are indissolubly connected with certain
sense-given phenomena. Now if we could discover
what are the motions which take place when we see
or hear or feel pain or pleasure, there is still a gap,
corresponding to his remark about the τὸ φαίνεσθαι.
Why a sensation of light should follow a motion in
the optic nerve, or pain or pleasure be connected with

certain changes in the organism, remains a mystery. That, in fact, is the difficulty which has been awaiting him all along. When he comes to his theory of human nature, he still tries to connect his doctrine with his general theory of motion in the nerves, but is forced to rely to some extent upon empirical psychology. He knows how men will act in given circumstances, not because he can deduce the action from any theory about the bodily organism, but because he observes that, as a matter of fact, such and such things are painful or pleasurable and lead to aversion and desire. He puts the case himself in a remarkable passage. The natural philosopher, as we have seen, must begin from geometry; "civil and moral philosophy" properly depend upon natural. But, he says, "the causes of the motions of the mind are known, not only by ratio-cination, but also by the experience of every man that takes the pains to observe those motions within him-self." Therefore we may either take the "synthetical method," and from "the very first principles of philo-sophy" deduce "the causes and necessity of creating commonwealths"; or, even without knowing geometry and physics, we may attain the principles of civil philosophy by the "analytical" method. The syn-thetical method proceeds from "motions of the mind"; the knowledge of these motions, again, follows from knowledge of "sense or imagination," and ultimately depends upon geometry. But the analytical method starts from a knowledge of law as dependent upon "power": of power as derived from the wills of the men "that constitute such power," and that again from a knowledge of men's appetites and passions. That knowledge is to be derived from every man's experience if he will but "examine his own mind." That is fortunate. If we had to deduce the nature of government and of right and wrong from geometry or physics, we should have to wait a long time for any satisfactory results. The materialist theory remains in Hobbes's mind as a self-evident truth, and has a very important influence upon his speculations. But his real method is different. That will appear hereafter.

H

CHAPTER III

MAN [1]

1. *Psychology*

MAN is a body with certain organs. Other bodies coming into contact with the organs of sense propagate motions through the nerves to the brain and heart. The reactions or "endeavours" set up in the central organs generate the sensations or phantasms which constitute the whole mental world. We are directly conscious of nothing else, although they enable us to perceive what happens "outside of the mind." The laws of motion, again, tell us that a thing once in motion "will be eternally in motion unless somewhat else stay it." "Whatever hindereth it will

---

[1] The second part of Hobbes's philosophy considered in this chapter is expounded in the early chapters of the *Leviathan* (vol. iii. of English works) and the *Human Nature*. The last, originally published in 1650, consists of the first thirteen chapters of the treatise written in 1640. The later part of the same treatise also appeared in 1650 as *De Corpore Politico*. These two form the fourth volume of the English works. A later treatise, *De Homine*, in Latin, appeared in 1658, but adds nothing to the earlier books. Hobbes never found himself able to give the fuller exposition which he had intended of the doctrines summarised in the *Human Nature* and the *Leviathan*; but he states the essence with sufficient terseness and clearness.

take some time to destroy the motion." "Though the wind cease, the waves give not over rolling for a long time after; so also it happeneth in that motion which is made in the internal parts of a man, then, when he sees, dreams, etc." The "image" thus formed remains for a time after the object is removed, and the faculty of retaining such images is therefore called "the imagination." Imagination is therefore "nothing but decaying sense." All knowledge and thought thus correspond to the action and reaction between the living body and the bodies which impinge upon it. Knowledge, therefore, is entirely constructed from experience, or from the action set up from outside, although the organised body has the power of reacting and so generating the phantasms which compose the "imaginary" or mental world. The problem which Hobbes now considers is how the mind or brain comes to systematise this varying play of imagery and to acquire both general truths and rules which govern conduct. We have already seen what is the logic which is worked out by the help of language; but we have also to consider man as an acting and feeling being. We must understand not only his methods of reasoning but the motives which govern his conduct.

Although Hobbes holds that the phantasms are caused by the internal motions, this cause does not really help us much to explain the effect. We have to look at the phantasms themselves. Hobbes is naturally much interested by the phenomena of dreaming, for dreams are entirely made up of phantasms. We catch the phantasms, so to speak, by themselves, shifting, combining, and behaving according to their own purpose. Sleep is a "privation of the act of sense." The power

to feel remains, but its activity is suspended for the
time.   Consequently the phantasms are not suppressed
or modified by the intrusion of images from without.
They are made up entirely of past images, though
combined in new and apparently arbitrary ways.
Sometimes they continue the train of images of the
waking state, but they also seem to spring up of
themselves.   The explanation is, that there is a
reciprocal action between the vital organs and the
phantasms.   "Sad imaginations nourish the spleen,
and a strong spleen reciprocally causeth fearful
dreams."   When we are awake fear causes cold, and
when we are asleep cold causes fear, and therefore
"dreams of ghosts."   This leads to an important
result which will meet us again.   Fear, "helped a
little with stories of such apparitions, causes guilty
men in the night and in hallowed places to see terrible
phantasms which they mistake for real ghosts and
incorporeal substances."   Our dreams are thus the
reverse of our waking imaginations, the motion when
we are awake beginning at one end, and when we
dream at the other.   The absence of interfering sensations, again, makes the phantasms as clear as the
waking impressions; and as they appear to be always
present and we do not remember or reflect, strange
things in dreams cause no wonder.   Finally, the incoherence of our dreams distinguishes them sufficiently
from the phantasms which, when we are awake, inform
us of a present reality.   When dreaming we do not
know that we are not awake, but when we are awake
we are quite sure that we are not dreaming.   "We do
not dream of the absurdities of our waking thoughts,"
but when awake we perceive the incoherence of our

dreams. In dreams "our thoughts appear like the
stars between flying clouds, not in the order in which
a man would choose to observe them, but as the
uncertain order of flying clouds permits."

What is it, then, that gives this colouring to our
waking thoughts? "Not every thought to every
thought succeeds indifferently." Our images are
relics of past sense impressions, and, moreover, they
succeed in the same order in which their originals
succeeded. One follows the other "as water upon
a plane table is drawn which way any one part is
guided by the finger." But we have experience of
images succeeding in the most various orders. There
is, therefore, no certainty as to what image will succeed
another at a given time, although it is certain that
the order is one in which we have previously experi-
enced them. Thus thoughts seem "impertinent to
one another" as in a dream. Yet even in this "wild
ranging of the mind" we may often perceive the
guiding cause. "For in a discourse of our present
civil war what could seem more impertinent than to
ask, as one did, what is the value of a Roman penny.
Yet the coherence to me was manifest enough. For
the thought of the war introduced the thought of the
delivering up of the king to his enemies; the thought
of that thought brought in the thought of the delivering up of Christ; and that again the thought of the
thirty pence, which was the price of that treason; and
thence easily followed that malicious question, and all
this in a moment of time, for thought is quick." This
passage, quoted by all critics of Hobbes, is a fine specimen of his pregnant style. G. H. Lewes remarks that
a popular rhetorician would have expanded the last

four words into a paragraph. A Scottish professor
would have proceeded to quote Akenside. It is also
remarkable as an illustration of the doctrine of the
"association of ideas" which was to become so prominent with Hobbes's successors. It has been pointed
out, indeed, that Hobbes was not the first person to
notice a phenomenon which had already been observed
by Aristotle. Nor has it with him the importance
which it assumed in later years. Hume declared
that the association of ideas was in mental phenomena
what gravitation was in astronomy, and Hartley's later
application of the doctrine to the moral as well as
the intellectual nature became the guiding principle
of the later empirical school in England. Hartley's
"vibratiuncles" play the same part as Hobbes's
"endeavours," and in both cases the physiological
theory, which professes to give the ground of the
phenomena, is rather deduced from the phenomena
themselves than independently ascertained. The
"association of ideas" remained when the vibratiuncles were dropped. To Hartley's followers it
seemed that the whole theory of knowledge depended
upon a thorough carrying out of this principle. Logic
in general seemed to them to be derivable from "association of ideas." Though Hobbes certainly did not
foresee this application of his statement, his use of the
observation is important. The "trains of thoughts,"
as he says, are of two kinds : the first is "unguided";
when thoughts are directed by association, and the
succession appears to be as casual as in a dream : the
second is "regulated by some desire or design." The
unregulated give us the kind of knowledge which
would be described by Hume as attributable to the

association of ideas. We remember things as ante-cedent and consequent, and this remembrance is an "experiment," whether made voluntarily, as when we put a thing in the fire to see what will happen, or "not made," as when we remember a fair morning after a cold evening. When we have often observed such a sequence we expect its repetition, and from this comes the kind of knowledge which we call "prudence." If the sign has preceded the event in a required number of cases, it may justify us in betting twenty to one that an event will happen, but never justifies a certainty, which belongs to science alone.

At this stage, then, cause and effect are represented simply by sequence—the sole meaning, according to the later empiricists, of cause and effect. Now when a man desires some end, he thinks of the means which will produce it. This kind of thinking Hobbes takes to be common to man and beast, though it is man alone who is capable of following the reverse method of deducing effects from causes. That method is peculiar to truly scientific reasoning. The "discourse of the mind," when directed by design, may lead to either process. A man has lost something, and his mind runs back from place to place and time to time to find when and where he had it, for he knows the place in which he is to seek, and "his thoughts run over all the parts thereof in the same manner as one would sweep a room to find a jewel, or as a spaniel ranges a field till he find a scent, or as a man should run over the alphabet to start a rhyme." In other cases a man comes to know what event will follow an action. He wishes to know, for example, what will be the consequence of committing a crime. He assumes that

like events will follow like actions; and so he thinks
of the sequence of "the crime, the officer, the prison,
the judge, and the gallows." That is a course of reflection which, as Hobbes undeniably says, is likely to
result in "prudence." Here again Hobbes emphasises
a distinction between "prudence" and "science," or
between merely empirical and necessary truth. He
therefore introduces at this point his theory of names
and "computation"—the method by which science is
elaborated. But when he is taking the psychological
rather than the logical view, and considering how as a
matter of fact knowledge is developed, he makes the
distinction less absolute. Science "after all" is a
development of "prudence."[1] Both kinds of knowledge, he says in the *Human Nature*, "are but experience," though science depends upon the "proper use of
names in language." This, however, implies the "con-
comitance of conception with words: for if words
alone were sufficient, a parrot might be taught as well
to know truth as to speak it. Evidence is to truth, as
the sap to the tree, which so far as it creepeth along
with the body and branches keepeth them alive; where
it forsaketh them, they die; for this evidence, which
is meaning with our words, is the life of truth." So
in the *Leviathan* he remarks that children before they
can speak are not properly reasonable, and most men
are little better. Having no science or knowledge of
consequences, they still resemble children, who are
made to believe that their new brothers and sisters
are found in the garden. Such natural "prudence,"
indeed, is better than false rules. "The light of

[1] See chapter vi. of *Human Nature*, and chapter v. of
Leviathan.

human reason is perspicuous words, but by exact
definitions first snuffed and purged from ambiguity.
Reason is the *pace*; increase of science the *way*; and
the benefit of mankind the *end.*" The ability of the
man who has natural dexterity with his weapon is to
the ability of the man who has thoroughly acquired
the art of fencing, as prudence to "sapience" (*sapientia*,
that is, or science). "Both (abilities) are useful; but
the latter infallible." Those, meanwhile, who trust to
books and follow the blind blindly are "like him that,
trusting to the false rules of a master of fence,
ventures presumptuously upon an adversary that
either kills or disgraces him." Thus in any business
where we have no "infallible science," it is better to
follow our "natural judgment than to be guided by
general sentences read in authors." Politicians love
to show their reading in councils, but very few do it
in their domestic affairs: having prudence enough at
home, though in "public they study more the reputation of their own wit than the success of another's
business." The accurate knowledge which comes with
a "proper use of names" is therefore, as it would seem,
not dependent upon "arbitrary conventions" as to
names, but a refinement and articulate organisation of
the simple conceptions out of which mere prudence or
a system of empirical knowledge is constructed.

Another point has now to be considered. Trains of
thought are "regulated" by the presence of some aim
or desire. The wild ranging of the mind represented
by dreams or mere "association of ideas" is then
directed to a single end. We have noticed sequences,
such as the crime, the prison, the gallows; and when we
desire, we think of the means which will produce the

desirable result, and then of the means to those means.
What then is a desire ? All conceptions and apparitions are really "motion in some internal substance of
the head." The motion "not stopping there but proceeding to the heart, of necessity must there either help
or hinder the motion which is called *vital*: when it
helpeth it is called *delight, contentment,* or *pleasure,* which
is nothing really but motion about the heart, as conception is nothing but motion in the head." When, on
the contrary, the vital motion is hindered, the hindering
motion is called pain. The physiology is of course
absurd, but the theory thus accepted is remarkable.
The same doctrine appears in Spinoza's *Ethics,* where
it becomes the foundation of his famous account of
the passions, held by many critics to be his masterpiece. Sir F. Pollock in his admirable exposition
observes that, according to Spinoza, "Pleasure marks
the rising and pain the lowering of the vital energies."
That phrase would serve equally as an equivalent
for the words just quoted from Hobbes. Sir F.
Pollock points out, again, that this doctrine has
been accepted by Mr. Herbert Spencer and other
modern thinkers. That pleasure and pain must in
some way correspond to heighten or lower vitality is
a doctrine which in some form or other becomes more
essential with the acceptance of evolution. It is quite
clear that while animals, human or other, seek for the
pleasurable and avoid the painful, a being which acted
upon the opposite plan would be in a very bad way.
A race which hated food and took delight in being
eaten would speedily be extinguished in the struggle
for existence. Spinoza bases his theory upon his
general principle—everything that is endeavours to

persist in its own being "*in suo esse perseverare conatur.*" Hobbes's acceptance of the law that the motion of a thing will persist unless altered by some other thing implies a perception of the same principle. Meanwhile he insists (in the *Human Nature*) upon another point of great importance.

"Ends," he says, may be near at hand or further off: those which are nearer are called "means" to the further. "But for an utmost end, in which the ancient philosophers have placed *felicity*, there is no such thing in this world, nor way to it, more than to Utopia: for while we live we have desires, and desire presupposeth a further end." There can, he infers, "be no contentment but in proceeding." We are not to marvel, therefore, when we see that as men attain to one end, "their appetite continually groweth" and they pursue some other. "Of those that have attained to the highest degree of honour and riches, some have affected mastery in some art; as Nero in music and poetry, Commodus in the art of a gladiator"; some kind of diversion, whether in play or business is still required; and men justly complain of a great grief that they know not what to do. "Felicity, therefore, by which we mean continual delight, consisteth *not* in having prospered but in prospering." This states a really valuable doctrine. Everything, we have seen, is motion: knowledge implies perpetual motion, the whole world-process is a continuous transformation of one system of motions into another; and life, of course, is essentially motion. To wish, therefore, for "Utopia," which excludes change, is to wish for something inconsistent with life and radically inconceivable. Hobbes constantly ridicules the scholastic doctrine of eternity as a "*nunc stans,*" a state which has no relation to time. That is one of his favourite illustrations of the use of meaningless words. The universe *is* change. He answers by anticipation an argument which finds favour with modern pessimists. Life, they suggest, is essentially misery, because we are always desiring, and desire implies want. The inference involves a fallacy. Time never stands still, and we are always moving on. We cannot sit down upon a solid lump of pleasure outside of time and change. We cannot imagine such a thing, for the words have no real meaning. Every end is also a beginning, and to think of the future is to desire. But desire is not necessarily painful. It does not imply dissatisfaction with the present, but only a hope that the change may lead in a certain direction. If the conditions of future fruition appear to be present, the expectation of change is itself delightful. We have, in Hobbes's language, appetites and aversions. Appetite is an endeavour towards an "object which delighteth." "Pleasure, love, and appetite are divers names for divers considerations of the same things." Opposed to "appetite" is "aversion," which "moves us when the object displeaseth." Happiness implies, therefore, such a process as involves a continuous activity of the vital powers and not an impossible and inconceivable state of changelessness. We cannot arrest time or cease the change, but we may be continually moving along the line of greatest vigour and happiness. This again seems to be often overlooked by Hobbes's disciples, the later utilitarians. Bentham is apt to talk about "lots" of happiness, as if happiness were a solid thing capable of being accumulated like coins in a bag. Life is a continuous process in which pain or pleasure may predominate, but its value is to be measured, not by the sum of things possessed, but by the nature of the energy evolved in possessing them.

This leads to Hobbes's theory of the passions, which, though characteristic, can hardly be described, like Spinoza's, as a "masterpiece." He has defined passion as "the motion about the heart," which is a consequence of "the motion of the brain," which we call conception. He has therefore "obliged himself to search out and declare from what conception proceedeth every one of the passions which are commonly taken notice of." The course of this inquiry is curious. He begins by a brief account of the sensual pains and pleasures. Among them are the pleasures of hearing. Galileo has done something towards explaining the pleasures of harmony; but "I confess that I know not," says Hobbes, "for what reason one succession in tone and measure is more pleasant than another." He conjectures that some airs imitate and revive a former passion; "for no air pleaseth but for a time, no more doth imitation." There is, however, "another delight by the ear," peculiar to musicians, namely, a "rejoicing of their own skill." Of this nature he says "are the passions of which I am to speak next." He is really dropping the attempt to give a scientific classification of the passions in order to dwell upon certain emotions interesting for the purpose of his political theories.

He begins from a sufficiently wide proposition. The expectation that anything will happen hereafter implies the knowledge that there is something present which has power to produce it; that knowledge being

derived from our remembrance of the past. "Where-
fore all conception of the future is conception of power
able to produce something. Whoever, therefore, ex-
pecteth pleasure to come must conceive withal some
power in himself by which the same may be attained."
When we desire a pleasure, we no doubt conceive ourselves to have the power of enjoying it. We may
perhaps desire something, while recognising that under
the circumstances it is impossible, as, according to the
poet, the moth may desire the star. But desire as
determining action, "the beginning of animal motion
towards something that pleaseth us," supposes that we
can enjoy and that we can act so as to procure the
enjoyment or the chance of it. This, however, does
not appear to throw much light upon the nature of
desire or of the special passions. Hobbes proceeds to
explain that by "power" he means all the faculties of
body and mind, and, besides these, all such further
power as is by them obtained, such as riches, authority,
friendship, and good fortune. However little the
general position can help us in "searching out" the
nature of the various passions, it shows what really
is in Hobbes's mind. Since man is a desiring animal,
and reaches one end only to anticipate further ends,
he seeks not only to gratify some particular passion,
but to obtain whatever may enable him to gain pleasure
and avoid pain of all kinds. He has various capacities for enjoyment, and necessarily desires all the power
which may enable him to go on enjoying as much as
possible. "Favour," riches, and so forth, are means
towards continuing a pleasant life. He adds a significant remark: "And because the power of one man
resisteth and hindereth the effects of the power of

another, *power* simply is no more but the *excess* of the
power of one above that of another; for equal powers
opposed destroy one another, and such opposition is
called *contention.*" It is clear that the meaning of
"power" has become restricted. It no longer means
anything which enables us to enjoy or to secure the
means of enjoyment, but that kind of power which
enables us to get a larger share than our neighbours.
He is not thinking, for example, of the power of per-
forming on the lute which gave him enjoyment when
he was locked up in his bedroom, but of the power
which enabled him to have a room to himself and keep
out the burglars who might have knocked him on the
head. Power is the ability of the individual to get as
large a share as possible of the good things that may
be going.

He proceeds to give definitions of a great number
of painful and pleasurable emotions. What we obtain
from him, however, is not properly a general theory
of the passions, but a not very systematic list of the
various emotions as determined by the relations between a man and the society in which he lives. Such
as it is, however, his list suggests to him a number
of characteristic and pungent sayings which have a
bearing upon his political theory, and are often, it must
be admitted, more forcible than edifying. The order
of exposition, I may remark, is clearer in the *Human
Nature* than in the *Leviathan.*

Since all desire implies desire for "power," the
recognition of the power belonging to ourselves or
others is an essential element in our relations to each
other. The "acknowledgment of power is called
Honour," and to honour a man is to conceive that he

has an "excess of power above him with whom he contendeth." All the signs of "power" are therefore honourable. Beauty of person or "general reputation among those of the other sex" is honourable as an indication of personal vigour. Actions which show strength of body, as victory in battle or duel, are honourable. *Avoir tué son homme* is an honour. So is a readiness to great exploits, for confidence gives a presumption of real power; and to teach is honourable as a sign of knowledge; and riches as a sign of the power that acquired them; and authority as a sign of the strength, wisdom, favour or riches by which it is acquired. Good fortune is honourable because a sign of the favour of God, to whom is to be ascribed all that cometh to us by fortune, no less than that we attain unto by industry. Gravity is honourable when a sign of "a mind employed on something else," employment being a sign of power. It is dishonourable when affected. For the gravity of the former kind is like a ship laden with merchandise, but of the latter like the steadiness of a ship ballasted with sand and other trash. Honour is the manifestation of the value we set on one another. The value or worth of a man is, as of all other things, his price : that is to say, as much as would be given for the use of his power; and therefore this value is not absolute, but a thing dependent on the need and judgment of another. So a good soldier is more valuable in war than in peace, while the reverse is true of a learned and uncorrupt judge. As in other things, so in men, not the seller but the buyer determines the price. For, let men, as most men do, rate themselves at the highest value they can, yet their true value is no more than it is esteemed

by others. Moreover, honour consisteth only in the
opinion of "power." If an action be great and difficult
and therefore a proof of great power, it matters not
whether it be just or unjust. The ancients thought
they were honouring their gods by ascribing to them
great though unjust acts; as in the Homeric hymn,
Mercury's greatest praise is that "being born in the
morning, he had invented music at noon, and before
night stolen away the cattle of Apollo." Piracy was
thought honourable by the Greeks, and at the present
time "private duels are and always will be honourable, though unlawful, till such time as there shall be
honour ordained for them that refuse, and ignominy
for them that make the challenge." Duels often show
courage, and therefore "strength and skill, which are
power," though for the most part, he admits, they are
the effects of rash speech and the "fear of dishonour."
Hobbes was the last man to insist that duelling should
be honoured; but that it was honoured is indisputable,
and he is simply considering the fact.

The desire for power implies the desire for honour:
the recognition of power by ourselves or others, for
that is itself power. We have next to notice the
passions which correspond to honour. The first is
"glory or internal gloriation or triumph of the mind."
This means the conception of our own power as compared with the power of "him that contendeth against
us." "By those whom it displeaseth this passion is
called pride; by those whom it pleaseth it is called a
just valuation of oneself." When the "imagination of
our power" arises from experience of our own actions,
it is just and well-grounded, and prompts aspiring to
higher degrees of power. When it arises from the

trusting other people's opinions, it becomes "false glory," and leads to mistaken ambition. Sometimes glory depends upon fiction, as when we imagine ourselves to be the hero of some romance. This begets no aspiration, and is "vain glory" when, "like the fly on the axletree, a man exclaims, 'What a dust do I raise.'" He illustrates it elsewhere from the gallant madness of Don Quixote, "which is nothing else but an expression of such height of vain glory as reading of romance may produce on pusillanimous men." It is shown by "affectation of fashions," and "usurping the signs of virtues" not really possessed. The opposite passion to glory is called "humility" by those by whom it is approved, and by others "dejection." "If well-grounded, it produceth fear to attempt anything rashly; if ill, it utterly cows a man, that he neither dares speak publicly nor expect success in any action."

Another passion of which Hobbes takes himself to have given the first explanation is marked by that "distortion of the countenance which we call laughter." The cause of laughter is not wit, "for men laugh at mischances and indecencies wherein there lieth no wit nor jest at all." What moves laughter must be something "new and unexpected." Men, especially if "greedy of applause," laugh at unexpected success in their actions and at their own jests. They laugh again at jests which elegantly discover the absurdity of another man. They do not laugh when they themselves or their friends are the objects of jesting. Laughter, then, is caused by "sudden glory": the discovery of some superiority in ourselves to other people. The popularity of this phrase shows, I fancy,

that Hobbes has more or less hit the mark.[1] It is
only fair to add his remark that the passion "is
incident most to them that are conscious of the fewest
abilities in themselves; who are forced to keep themselves in their own favour by observing the imper-
fections of other men. And therefore much laughter
at the defects of others is a sign of pusillanimity.
For of great minds one of the proper works is to
help and free others from scorn, and compare themselves only with the most able." We should only
laugh "when all the company may laugh together,"
as "at absurdities abstracted from persons." That
is a fair test of the innocence of laughter, with which
Chesterfield might agree.

The attempt to analyse the passions into some form
of the desire for power or honour has less edifying
consequences. Hobbes, we discover, is the most
thoroughgoing of egoists, and not only admits the
universality of self-love, but speaks as though this
were one of the obvious truths which require no
proof or explanation. "Pity," he observes with superlative calmness, is imagination or fiction of future
calamity to ourselves, proceeding from the sense of
another man's calamity. We pity those who suffer
an undeserved calamity, "because then there appeareth
more probability that the same may happen to us:
for the evil that happeneth to an innocent man
may happen to every man." That is why men pity
those whom they love; for whom they love they think
worthy of good and therefore not worthy of calamity.
This may suggest the question, "What is the meaning

[1] It is discussed by Professor Sully in his recent book upon
humour.

of love ?" He discusses this in the *Human Nature*,
though he apparently does not think it worthy of consideration in the *Leviathan*. Love in the most general
sense means simply the "delight" caused by an object
which helps the vital motion, hatred having the corresponding relation to pain. This, he says, sufficiently
explains the love which men have to one another, or
the pleasure which they take in each other's company,
which entitles them to be called "sociable." To love
men means that we think of them as useful. Of love
in the narrower sense, or the passion which is "the
great theme of poets," he observes that, in spite of
their "praises," it means the lover's "need," not any
special quality in the object beloved. "Those are
most successful in love who care least, which not perceiving many men cast away their services as one arrow
after another till, in the end, together with their hopes
they lose their wits." Hobbes is not very clear at this
point—perhaps he was a little shy of "the poets"—
but he does not appear to take a romantic view of the
question. Another variety of love is more properly
called "good will or charity." This is a modification,
again, of the desire for power. Nothing can convince
a man of his own power more completely than the
discovery that he is able not only to accomplish his
own desires but also to assist other men in theirs.
This is the secret of "the natural affection of parents to
their children (which the Greeks call στοργή)," as also of
the affection implied in "assisting those who adhere to
us." When, however, men bestow benefits upon
strangers, they do not act from charity; but either
seek to "purchase friendship" by contract, or seek
peace from fear. We act for the good of others, it

seems, either from the complacency derived from the evidence of our own power, which is properly "charity," or in order to buy their services. Hobbes speaks as if his view were not only obvious, but edifying—as though he were simply elaborating St. Paul's famous description of the Christian virtue of charity.

Another passion is more intelligible to him. Since "knowledge is power," we naturally desire to extend our knowledge. The corresponding passion is called "admiration," and the "appetite" is "curiosity." Its existence, like the faculty of language, marks the point at which we part company from beasts. The beast flies from or approaches a new object, only considering whether it will "serve his turn." The man endeavours to discover the cause. Hence arises all philosophy, which is, as we know, the theory of consequences in general. A man in chase of riches or power ("which in respect of knowledge are but sensuality") does not care about the motions of the stars: it is only a few, as he remarks elsewhere, who appreciate science, "for science is of that nature as none can understand it to be, except such as in a good measure have attained unto it." The military arts are of obvious utility and their possessors are powerful. "Though the true mother of them be science, namely the mathematics; yet because they are brought into light by the hand of the artificer, they be esteemed (the mid-wife passing with the vulgar for the mother) as his issue." Hobbes can preach with feeling on the superiority of philosophical inquiry to the mere bread-winning studies. Meanwhile "curiosity is delight; therefore also novelty is so; but especially that novelty from which a man conceiveth an opinion true or false of bettering his estate ; for in such case they stand affected with the hope that all gamesters have while the cards are shuffling." That no doubt expresses a very genuine sentiment. Though science is power, he would say, the man of science has very little honour, unless he can apply his science to generally intelligible ends. "Curiosity" and reason distinguish man from beasts; "which makes me, when I hear a man upon the discovery of any new and ingenious knowledge or invention ask gravely, that is to say scornfully, *what 'tis good for*, meaning what money it will bring in, to esteem that man not sufficiently removed from brutality." Love of philosophic truth, one is glad to observe, appears to Hobbes to be admirable for itself, though perhaps at some cost of consistency.

The curious argument which follows is of some interest. What, he asks, is the cause of the great difference between men's capacities ? It cannot be a difference in the "natural temper of the brain" for, if so, the difference would show itself "in the senses"; whereas wise men and foolish have (as he assumes) equal senses. Imagination being "decaying sense," the imagination ought to be equal. The difference is therefore owing to the differences in the constitution " of the body." What helps the "vital constitution" in one man, and is therefore pleasurable, hinders it in another, and is therefore painful. He discusses the "intellectual virtues"—meaning, the qualities which are desired "for eminence " and are gauged by "comparison"; for "if all things were equal in all men, nothing would be prized." The great difference between men's wits is due to a difference in "quick-

ness," or " swift succession of one thought to
another," and in "steadiness of direction to some
approved end." A defect of quickness is " dullness or
stupidity"; and the difference is due to the difference
of the passions. Desire for power, riches, knowledge,
or honour (the last three being modifications of the
first) is thus the great cause of the "difference of wit."
A man who has no great passion for any of these things
may be good in the sense of inoffensive ; "yet he cannot possibly have either a great fancy or much judgment. For the thoughts are to the desires as scouts
and spies, to range abroad and find the way to the
things desired—all steadiness of the mind's motion and
all quickness of the same proceeding from thence ; for
as to have no desire is to be dead, so to have weak
passions is dullness ; and to have passions indifferently
for everything is giddiness and distraction"; while
abnormal vehemence of passion is madness. That
intellectual excellence is dependent upon the character
and the strength of the emotions is a doctrine upon
which Hobbes rightly and impressively insists. Fancy,
according to him, means quickness in perceiving "similitudes"; and judgment or "discretion" quickness in perceiving "dissimilitudes." Fancy must be "eminent"
in poetry, though judgment is required ; while in history fancy is wanted only to "adorn the style." In
demonstration, "judgment does all," except that "an
apt similitude" may be required to open the understanding. "Discretion" is required in poetry ; an "an-
atomist or physician" may speak of "unclean things";
"but for another man to write his extravagant or
pleasant fancies of the same is as if a man from being
tumbled in the dirt should come and present himself

before good company." This is a doctrine for which
Hobbes might have found plenty of contemporary
and other illustrations. An excessive "mobility of
mind," again, maketh men depart "from their discourse by a parenthesis, and from that parenthesis by
another, till at length they either lose themselves, or
make their narration like a dream or some studied
nonsense." He would not have enjoyed *Sordello*.
"Madness" is a general name for "all passions that
produce strange and unusual behaviour." It is especially conspicuous in a multitude, he says, answering by
anticipation a famous query of Bishop Butler. "For
what argument of madness can there be greater than
to clamour, strike, and throw stones at our best friends?
Yet this is somewhat less than such a multitude will do.
For they will clamour, fight against, and destroy those
by whom all their lifetime before they have been protected and secured from injury. And if this be madness in the multitude, it is the same in every particular
man." Each particle of water "contributes as much to
the roaring of the sea" as any other drop, and the
same is true of the "seditious roaring of a troubled
nation."

Such remarks, though characteristic, are more or
less digressions from the main purpose, to which he
returns in a chapter upon "the difference of manners"
in the *Leviathan*. By manners, he tells us, he does not
mean "points of the *small morals*"—social etiquette—
but the qualities of mankind that concern their living
together in "peace and unity." In other words, he
will ask how the passions of the individual bear upon
the political order. Since felicity, as we have seen,
"is a continual progress of the desire from one object

to the other," all men desire both to procure and
assure a contented life. Unluckily they differ as to the
way, from the diversity of passions or difference in
knowledge. In the first place, therefore, he will
"put for a general inclination of all mankind, a perpetual and restless desire of power after power, that
endeth only in death." It is not that a man can
always hope for a greater delight, but because he cannot be assured of "the means to live which he hath
at present without the acquisition of more." "Competition of riches, honour, command, or other power
inclineth to contention, enmity, and war; because the
way of one competitor to the attaining of his desire is
to kill, subdue, supplant, or repel the other." Particularly "competition of praise," as he rather oddly
adds, "inclineth to a reverence of antiquity. For men
contend with the living, not with the dead; to these
ascribing more than due, that they may obscure the
glory of the other." Desire of "ease" disposeth men
to obedience, and so does desire of knowledge and the
arts of peace, for such desire "containeth a desire of
leisure." Desire of fame "disposeth to laudable actions,"
even of "fame after death." For though after death
we have no sense of praise on earth, men have a
present delight therein from foresight of it, and of
the benefit to their posterity; which though they see
not, yet they "imagine," and everything that is a
pleasure to the sense, the same also is pleasure in the
imagination. Receiving benefits from an equal "disposeth to counterfeit love, but really secret hatred;
and puts a man into the estate of a desperate debtor
that, in declining the sight of his creditor, tacitly
wishes him there where he might never see him more.

For benefits oblige, and obligation is thraldom ; and
an unrequitable obligation perpetual thraldom, which
is to one's equal hateful." Obligation to a recognised
superior, however, "inclines to love," for it can be
requited by gratitude, and so long as there is a hope
of requital, we are disposed to love even an equal
or inferior benefactor ; the obligation is then mutual ;
"from whence proceedeth an emulation of who shall
exceed in benefiting ; the most noble and profitable
contention possible ; wherein the victor is pleased
with his victory, and the other revenged by confessing
it." Ignorance "disposeth men to take on trust not
only the truth they know not, but also the errors and,
which is more, the nonsense of them they trust."
Ignorance of the nature of right, in particular, "disposeth a man to think that unjust which it hath been
the custom to punish, and that just, of the impunity
and approbation whereof they can produce an example
or, as the lawyers, which only use this false measure of
justice, barbarously call it, a precedent." Such men "set
themselves against reason as often as reason is against
them ; which is the cause that the doctrine of right
and wrong is perpetually disputed both by the pen
and the sword ; whereas the doctrine of lines and
figures is not so." Truth in geometry "crosses no
man's ambition, profit, or lust." "For I doubt not but
if it had been a thing contrary to any man's right of
dominion, or to the interest of men that have dominion,
*that the three angles of a triangle should be equal to two
angles of a square*, that doctrine should have been, if not
disputed, yet by the burning of all books of geometry
suppressed, as far as he whom it concerned was
able."

The quaint passage in the *Human Nature* which
concludes this account of the passions sums up his
view. Life, he says, may be compared to a race—
a race which has no other " goal " or " garland " than
"being foremost." " In it to endeavour is *appetite*; to
be remiss is *sensuality* : to consider them behind is
glory : to consider them before is *humility* : . . . to fall
on the sudden is disposition to *weep* : to see another
fall is disposition to *laugh* : to see one outgone whom
we would not, is *pity* : to see one outgo whom we
would not is *indignation* : to hold fast by another is
love : to carry him on that so holdeth is *charity* : to
hurt oneself for haste is *shame* : . . . continually to be
outgone is *misery* : continually to outgo the next before
is *felicity* : and to forsake the course is to *die*."

Life, we see, is essentially competition, though as
yet the struggle for existence is regarded as only
affecting the individual. Hobbes, it will probably
appear to most people, takes a sufficiently cynical view
of human nature. He has been compared to Roche-
foucauld, though he does not represent the epigram-
matic skill which is gained in highly polished society.
He has frequented Mersenne's " cell," not the courtier's
salon. His opinions might be compared to the so-called
Machiavellianism of Bacon's essays—the concentration
of the experience of the statesman and lawyer, who
wishes to see things as they are and to get rid of
humbug and conventional gloss. Hobbes, however,
has a more distinctly scientific aim, and wishes at least
to connect his remarks with psychological theory. He
would defend himself against the charge that he is taking an "unworthy" view of mankind by appealing to
plain facts. Men, he would say, are stupid and selfish.

That, no doubt, is not the way to be popular. The "idealist" often takes a more painful view of men as they are, than the poor "cynic"; but he atones for it by an enthusiastic view of what they may become, and his readers catch the contagion of his enthusiasm. Their perception of the general corruption convinces them that they at any rate are of the salt of the earth, and this is comforting. If Hobbes's cynicism meant simply that he recognised the great part played by dullness and selfishness in human affairs, and the futility of overlooking that fact in political theories, we might say that he was applying a wholesome corrective to extravagant belief in millenniums.

It must be granted, however, that he goes beyond this. His quiet resolution of all the virtues into forms of egoism was of course condemned by the respectable. In our eyes it may be redeemed by the charming simplicity and utter unconsciousness of offence with which he propounds his atrocious theories. He becomes unintentionally humorous. We must, however, notice the nature of the reasoning which leads him to such conclusions. That is implied by one characteristic doctrine. Every man, he says, calls that which pleaseth him good, and that which displeaseth him evil. Since men differ in "constitution," they differ as to what is good and what is evil. There is no such thing as "absolute goodness considered without relation." Even God's goodness means His goodness to us. The words "good" and "evil," he says elsewhere, "are ever used with reference to us." No "common rule" can be taken "from the nature of the objects themselves." Such a rule must be made by the man himself, or by the "commonwealth," or by

some arbitrator set up by consent. It is indeed quite
clear that from Hobbes's point of view the abstract
words "good" and "evil" could have no meaning.
As "man" only means John and Thomas and Peter,
"good" only means what John and Thomas and Peter
like, and "evil" what they dislike. Moreover, if
psychological and ethical theories are to be based upon
experience, we must begin by studying the likings and
dislikings of human beings. Science must start from
the actual not from the ideal. A scientific theory of
human nature begins from the question, what passions
do in fact govern, not from the question what passions
ought to govern, human beings. Now in fact men
have various passions and desires which lead them to
break as well as to obey rules of morality. In a
dozen men we may find a Judas Iscariot as well as a
St. John; and we have to account equally for both.
As a physiologist has to deal with the morbid as well
as the healthy, so the psychologist has to deal with
the traitor as well as the saint, and with all the complex play of good and bad impulses, which make saints
and criminals and men of every intervening shade.
He will of course admit that, as a fact, a certain moral
code comes into existence, conformity to which is
regarded with approval by the average man. How it
comes to be formed, and what is the nature of its
authority, are questions to which Hobbes addresses
himself in the political treatises, and of which he offers
a very remarkable solution.

Hobbes can only say at present, that, since each
man is governed by his own passions and desires,
the formation of the "common rule" supposes some
"arbitrator" or central authority. His uncompro-

mising egoism is an inevitable consequence of his
position. It is assumed by the moralists whom he
attacked that there is some ultimate and absolute
good : an ideal law revealed through reason and
equally binding upon all men. It determines conduct, since the will always chooses the "apparent
good." Reason is itself virtue, and vice means ignorance, for it is only from a mistaken view of what is
really good that men fail to do right. Hobbes might
agree with the doctrine that man always chooses the
apparent good ; but he denies that the really good is
knowable. The doctrine therefore means for him
that each man will do what is pleasant to himself.
He is governed exclusively by his own desires, and it
would be as absurd to speak of a man acting from
another man's motives as to speak of his body being
nourished by another man's food. Now it must be
observed that later thinkers, who profess equally to
base ethical theories entirely upon experience, will not
admit this conclusion. They hold that sympathy is a
genuine and ultimate emotion ; and that man can so
identify himself with the society of which he forms a
part, that public spirit or patriotism or philanthropy
or family affection may be as genuine a motive as the
animal appetites. They hold, and, as I think, rightly,
that an empirical theory of morality does not really
involve the acceptance of a selfish or egoistic doctrine.
But it is undeniable that this interpretation is plausible.
The utilitarians could argue with great force that a
tendency to produce the "greatest happiness of the
greatest number" gives the true criterion of morality.
But, as an historical fact, they found their greatest
difficulty in reconciling this with their other assump-

tion, that each man seeks his own happiness. They
tried to explain "altruism" by "association," at the
risk of making it a kind of desirable fallacy, or else
they tried to show—what unfortunately cannot be
shown—that self-sacrifice is always repaid or, in other
words, is a sham sacrifice.

Hobbes had not to bother himself about such con-
ciliation. He was perfectly content to profess the
most unblushing egoism and carry it out consistently.
His essential aim was to be scientific, to accept the
obvious facts, and to carry out the conclusions logically. His nominalism naturally went with individual-
ism. Each man obviously is a separate thing which
must be explained by its own properties, and not by
reference to any mysterious bond of unity with other
things. Unfortunately there is selfishness enough in
the world to give much plausibility to some of his
statements, and to admit of their being often approximately true. Finally, his thorough materialism seems
to make the assumption of selfishness inevitable. If,
indeed, it be possible to regard man as a mere mechanism, worked by the laws of motion, and yet to regard
him as a self-conscious, reasoning, and remembering
animal, it may also be possible to regard him as
sympathetic and unselfish. Still it is difficult to see
how the actions of a mere automaton, affected only by
the pressure of bodies in contact with him, can be
really determined by the conditions of other automata.
He may be so constituted as to preserve his own
equilibrium; but his relation to his like would seem
to be limited to the cases in which two automata knock
their heads together. Hobbes, however, had no difficulty in altogether denying the existence of sympathy.

The desire for self-preservation was quite enough to
provide the working force for his scheme; and he
propounds his theory with the straightforward blunt-
ness which has the charm of obvious sincerity.

2. *Theology.*

We are now pretty well prepared to proceed to the
third part of Hobbes's philosophy; but there are two
other applications of his first principles which have a
bearing upon his political doctrine, and which also
deserve consideration for themselves. We have seen
what Hobbes thought of bodies; we may ask what was
his creed as to the creator of bodies and the relation
of the creator to man? His arguments upon theology
and upon the problem of free-will excited the keenest
antagonism among his contemporaries. His position in
both cases is remarkable, if only as illustrating the
stir which he gave to thought in general. Whether
his teaching was right or wrong, or a little of both, it
at least caused his opponents to look into the foundations of their own creed.

Hobbes steadily denied that the name "atheist"
properly applied to him. He calls himself not only a
theist, but a Christian, and even a faithful member of
the Church of England. Some of his critics accept
his assurances so far as to hold that he only meant to
reject scholastic dogmas or "incrustations," and did
not get beyond what is vaguely called Socinianism, or,
perhaps, "unsectarian Christianity." In such discussions two distinct questions are apt to be confounded.
The question, that is, what a man really believed, is
identified with the question what were the logical con-

sequences of his belief. It is undeniable that a man often rejects, and sometimes rejects with horror, doctrines which to others seem to be inevitable inferences from the first principles which he explicitly affirms. It is therefore " unfair," we are told, to attribute to a man the beliefs which, to our minds, he was logically bound to hold. It is certainly unfair so far as it is false. If a man repudiates a doctrine, the repudiation should be noted, even though we may think that he is under a delusion, which amounts to a concealment of his own opinions from himself under a jugglery of words. Sometimes, indeed, we are only "unfair" in the sense that we are paying him too high a compliment by supposing that he saw the full bearing of his arguments. It is no doubt unfair again to impute opinions which a man disavows, when they are opinions which will incur odium, or perhaps involve a probability of being burnt. If the bishops, of whom Hobbes was afraid, had refused to take notice of his repudiation of atheism, they would certainly have been unjust. We have not now, however, to consider whether Hobbes deserved either burning or damnation. The devoutest of bishops would not have the least wish to burn him at the present day, and we generally admit that opinions, honestly entertained for their supposed reasonableness, do not justify moral reprobation. Our duty to Hobbes personally is simply the duty of ascertaining what, as a fact, he did think, or thought that he thought. It is of some importance to know what he thought if we wish to estimate his character for honesty and courage. But for us the more important question is what were the true logical bearings of his position, whether he perceived them or not. Those

were what really affected the thought of his time.
When you have once started an argument, you cannot
tell what effect it will have upon others. You are
firing a charge of dynamite, and the explosion will act
irrespectively of the man who set it going. The first
and most important question is what "Hobbism"
means, whether Hobbes meant it or not. When we
know that, we can draw such inferences as seem
reasonable as to his personal character.

In his *Objections* to Descartes, Hobbes indicates
very plainly his position in regard to theology. He
criticises Descartes's famous argument that the "idea"
of God as a perfect being necessarily implies also
God's existence. Hobbes replies summarily that we
have no "idea" of God. An idea according to him is,
as we have seen, nothing but "decaying sense." It is
a fading picture of some object previously perceived
by the hands, eyes, or ears. Now nobody, of course,
could ever have supposed that "God" could be perceived in that way. Descartes answers that by
"idea" he means something entirely different from
Hobbes's "idea." What he meant need not be inquired,
and Hobbes did not take the trouble to inquire. He
takes it for granted that all knowledge of facts comes
to us through the senses, and that the *a priori* method
without appeal to experiences must be sterile. That
is to him too obvious to need proof. If so, it would
seem that demonstrations of the existence of God are
impossible. "Knowable" means visible or tangible,
and God is admittedly neither. Hobbes, however,
does not admit this conclusion. After discussing
man's knowledge and passions as related to "natural
things," he assumes that we also give names to (that

is, reason about) "things supernatural," that is God
and spirits. Such names ought to correspond to some
reality, and their meaning will explain in what sense
we use the phrases ascribing certain attributes to the
beings named. The belief in things supernatural is
produced by "curiosity," that is, as he explains, "love
of the knowledge of causes." This leads a man to ask
the cause of an effect; "and, again, the cause of that
cause; till of necessity he must come to this thought
at last that there is some cause, whereof there is no
former cause, but is eternal; which is it men call God;
so that it is impossible to make any profound inquiry
into natural causes, without being inclined thereby to
believe there is one God eternal." God is the first
"power of all powers, and first cause of all causes."
The name implies "eternity, incomprehensibility, and
omnipotency." Incomprehensibility is explained by
an analogy. A man born blind, when he warms himself by the fire, may convince himself that there is
something there which is called fire by his companions,
and which is the cause of the heat which he feels.
But he cannot have any such "idea" of it as those
have that see it. "So also by the visible things in
this world, and their admirable order, a man may
conceive there is a cause of them, which men call God,
and yet not have an idea or image of him in his mind."
The attributes of this Being must also be inconceivable. We speak of God as "seeing, hearing, speaking,
knowing, loving, and the like," names which have a
meaning as applied to men, but mean "nothing in the
nature of God." It is "well reasoned, shall not the
God that made the eye see, and the ear hear?" But it
is also well reasoned "if we say, shall God which

made the eye, not see without the eye ; or that made
the ear, not hear without the ear ; or that made the
brain, not know without the brain ; or that made the
heart, not love without the heart." The attributes of
God signify "our incapacity" or "our reverence":
our "incapacity when we say *incomprehensible* and
infinite; our reverence when we give him those names
which amongst us are the names of those things we
most magnify and commend, as omnipotent, omnisci-
ent, just, merciful, etc."

This may remind us of many controversies in which
some orthodox divines have agreed with Hobbes.
It recalls, for example, the agnosticism which
Mr. Herbert Spencer professes himself to have expanded from Sir William Hamilton ; while Mansel
used the same doctrine in defence of orthodox creeds.
So far Hobbes might have agreed with Mansel rather
than with Mr. Spencer, and might have believed
his creed to be susceptible of an interpretation
reconcilable with orthodoxy. His position, however,
depends upon his theory of causation. Although
he speaks of the "admirable order" of the world, he
emphatically rejects the doctrine of final causes. We
are not to infer from the eye or the ear any likeness
between the Creator and his creature ; but only some
inscrutable cause. And if we take into account what
Hobbes meant by cause we come to a difficulty. The
whole "world-process," according to him, is simply a
series of changes in motion : when we inquire into the
cause of any event we are really asking what was the
previous state of things from which the succeeding was
developed by a continuous series of change according
to purely mechanical laws. The "cause" of the

present arrangement of the stars is simply their preceding arrangement. The argument, therefore, for a first cause means, on his interpretation, that we cannot continue this inquiry indefinitely. Instead of saying "this state implies a preceding state," "we must say "this state implies that it was put together supernaturally."

Now in the *De Corpore* he criticises this argument himself. A man will be "wearied," he says, in tracing back the series of cause and effect, and "give over" inquiry. "But,whether we suppose the world to be finite or infinite, no absurdity will follow." "As it is true that nothing is moved by itself, so it is true also that nothing is moved but by that which was already moved." That implies an indefinite regress. "I cannot therefore commend," he says, "those that boast they have demonstrated by reasons drawn from natural things that the world had a beginning. They are contemned by idiots because they understand them not; and by the learned, because they understand them; by both deservedly." "They are entangled," he says "in the words *infinite* and *eternal*, of which we have in our mind no idea but that of our own insufficiency to comprehend them," and thus they are forced "either to speak something absurd, or, which they love worse, to hold their peace." Infinite, in short, means simply indefinitely great. Hobbes, therefore, will be content "with that doctrine concerning the beginning and magnitude of the world which I have been persuaded to by the Holy Scriptures, and fame of the miracles which confirm them; and by the custom of my country and reverence due to the laws."

These may be excellent, but are scarcely philo-

sophical, reasons. Bramhall, when he accused Hobbes
of atheism, refers to this passage. Hobbes, he says,
denies that there is any "argument to prove a Deity,"
except the creation of the world, and that the question
whether the world had a beginning must be settled
"not by argument, but by the magistrate's authority."
Hobbes replies that it may be settled "by the
Scriptures." "As far as arguments from natural
reason," he adds, "neither you nor any other have
hitherto brought any, except the creation, that has
not made it more doubtful to many men than it was
before." He then repeats the passage just quoted
from the *De Corpore*, and adds :—"This, doctor, is not
ill said, and yet it is all you ground your slander on,
which you make to sneak vilely under a crooked
paraphrase." "These opinions [about the beginning
of the world, apparently] are to be judged by those to
whom God has committed the ordering of religion;
that is, to the supreme governors of the Church; that
is, in England, to the king." Charles II. apparently
was to decide whether the world had a beginning.

Putting aside for the moment this quaint transi-
tion from reason to the British Constitution, it is to
be noticed that Hobbes had expressed himself unequi-
vocally in the *De Cive* and the *Leviathan*. By God, he
says, is understood the cause of the world. "To say
the world is God, is to say there is no cause of it, that
is, no God. . . . To say the world was not created but
eternal, seeing that which is eternal has no cause, is
to deny there is a God." It is plain then that if we
may put these statements together, Hobbes declares
that the only proof of God's existence is the creation
of the world, and that we cannot possibly know

whether the world was or was not created. In any
case, as we have seen, Hobbes always asserts most
emphatically that we really know nothing of God's
attributes, except His existence. Other attributes are
negative or metaphorical or signs of "honour." We
know nothing of God's "natural kingdom" except
"from the principles of natural science, which are so
far from teaching us anything of God's nature, as they
cannot teach us our own nature nor the nature of the
smallest creature living. And therefore when men out
of the principles of natural reason dispute of the
attributes of God, they but dishonour him; for in the
attributes which we give to God we are not to consider
the signification of philosophical truth, but the signification of pious intention to do him the greatest honour
we are able." Existence indeed implies something
more. Hobbes, as we have seen, denies that spirits are
"incorporeal"; to say that a spirit is an "incorporeal
substance" is to say that there is no spirit at all.
Bramhall says that the same would apply to God.
Hobbes replies that the true question is "whether
God be a phantasm (*id est* an idol of the fancy, which
St. Paul saith is nothing) or a corporeal spirit, that is
to say, something that has magnitude." He therefore
holds that God is a "most pure, simple, invisible,
spirit corporeal." He illustrates this by a strange
analogy. He has seen "two waters, one of the river,
the other a mineral water, so like that no man could
discern the one from the other," and yet when mixed,
the whole was indistinguishable in appearance from
milk. "If then such gross bodies have so great
activity, what shall we think of spirits, whose kinds
be as many as there be kinds of liquor, and activity

greater?" (How does he know that?) "Can it
then be doubted that God, who is an infinitely fine
spirit and withal intelligent, can make and change
all kinds of bodies as he pleaseth?" God, then,
like other spirits, is corporeal, though he may be
called "incorporeal" to imply that he is "something
between *infinitely subtile* and *nothing*: less subtile
than infinitely subtile, and yet more subtile than a
thought." It would be superfluous to examine this
singular hypothesis to which Hobbes is driven by his
desire to reconcile his materialism with his theology.
It is enough to remark that his system would clearly
be more consistent and intelligible if he simply omitted
the theology altogether.

Meanwhile Hobbes has another doctrine about
theology which is of more interest and more in accordance with his general theories. Religion, he says, is
peculiar to man, and its "seed" is therefore in some
quality peculiar to him. Such a quality is his curiosity
as to causes; and though men vary, all men are "curious
in the search of the causes of their own good and evil
fortune." When he cannot discover true causes, a
man supposes such as are suggested by his fancy.
Meanwhile his desire for security puts him in a state
of "perpetual solicitude." He resembles Prometheus
on the Caucasus, "a place of large prospect," though
far from comfortable. He hath "his heart all the day
long gnawed on by fear of death, poverty, or other
calamity; and has no repose nor pause of his anxiety
but in sleep." The fear creates its object, as it does,
according to his previous remark, in the case of
dreams. Men ignorant of causes have to invent "some
power or agent invisible." It is thus true that the

gods of the Gentiles "were at first created by human
fear." Men could not, again, make any other guess
as to the substance of these agents than that it was
"the same with that of the soul of man," and that
the soul of man was of the same substance with that
which appears in a dream to sleepers or in a looking-
glass to men awake. These they took for "real
external substances," and called them ghosts, that
is "thin aerial bodies"—for nobody could think
them really "incorporeal." This ignorance, again, led
them to guess at omens and prognostics when they
observed accidental coincidences which they took to
imply real connections. Naturally they guessed these
agents to resemble themselves, and pacified them by
gifts and prayers. Hobbes has already noted that
from the difficulty of distinguishing "dreams and
other strong fancies from vision and sense" arose the
old worship of satyrs, fauns, nymphs, and the like, and
nowadays the opinion that rude people have of fairies,
ghosts, and goblins, and the power of witches.
(Witches, he has to interject, are rightly punished,
because they believe in their own power of doing
mischief, not that "witchcraft is any real power.")
Belief in fancies and ghosts is inculcated to keep in
credit the use of exorcism, of crosses, of holy water,
and other such inventions of "ghostly men." "In
these four things, opinion of ghosts, ignorance of
second causes, devotion towards what men fear, and
taking of things casual for prognostics, consisteth the
natural seed of *religion*." The seeds have been
cultivated by "two sorts of men": by founders of
commonwealths and the lawgivers of the Gentiles on
the one hand, who "used their own invention," and

on the other by "Abraham, Moses, and our blessed
Saviour," who acted by "God's commandment and
direction." Both desired to make men more apt to
obedience, laws, peace, charity, and civil society;
though in one case religion was part of "human
politics," and in the other of "divine politics." He
has then no difficulty in showing what grotesque
results followed from the Gentile religions; and when
Bramhall founds upon this passage a charge of
atheism, he can reply that his account of the origin
of religion tells against the Gentile superstitions alone.
The savage people feared "invisible powers," that is,
something which they took to be gods; so that the
fear of a god, though not the true one, was to them
the beginning of religion, as the fear of the true
God was the beginning of wisdom to the Jews and
Christians.

The political aspect of his theory which makes
legislators the founders of religion will be noticed
presently. In the *Leviathan* he gives some remarkable definitions: "Fear of power invisible feigned
by the mind or imagined from tales publicly allowed
—*Religion*; not allowed—*Superstition*; and when the
power imagined is truly such as we imagine—
True Religion." "True religion," it may be inferred,
when not publicly allowed, is superstition. Whether
Hobbes wishes to draw that inference we need not
decide, nor need we ask how far he was quite convinced that the history of the Jewish belief presents
so complete a contrast to the history of the religions
founded by other legislators.

It is enough to say that Hobbes is here on the way
to much later speculation. A hundred years afterwards

Hume in his *Natural History of Religion* treated the same topic with his usual acuteness, and suggested theories afterwards taken up by Comte. Later students of the science of religion have enormously extended the range of the inquiry and accumulated vast masses of evidence for various theories. In Hobbes's time, or, indeed, in Hume's or even Comte's, it was not possible to get beyond general conjectures. Hobbes knew next to nothing of the savage peoples to whom he refers, and can only guess as to their probable mode of thought. He is thinking chiefly of the classical mythologies, where he can find plenty of examples of grotesque and vicious deities. All that can be said is, that he saw clearly the importance of the problems as to the growth of religions, though, in the absence of the requisite knowledge, he could only make a few very acute and pithy suggestions.

If we now come to the question what was Hobbes's real position in regard to theology, I think that there can be only one answer. It is quite clear that his, like other materialistic systems, is incompatible with anything that can be called theism. His argument comes merely to this, that if the world was created— a point which, we see, he admits to be doubtful—the Creator must have been a Being of stupendous power, but one of whom we are unable to say anything else. The doctrine that he is "corporeal" or an infinitely "subtile" matter occupying space is merely a quaint attempt to evade the more natural inference that he is simply outside of all knowable relations. A religion of this kind is not likely to give much trouble to anybody; and Hobbes's opponents were right in regarding him as virtually opposed to all possible

theology. What Hobbes himself thought is not quite
so obvious. There is a presumption, indeed, that so
bold a thinker must have seen the plain inferences
from his principles. If he did not see them for himself, they were pointed out by antagonists; and though
Hobbes, like most people, was apt to think that
antagonism means misrepresentation, he could scarcely
fail to see that they had in his case some ground for
their comments. His answers, indeed, seem less to
meet the arguments than to be ingenious devices for
shifting the question. Hobbes certainly made his
reserves. When Spinoza's *Tractatus Theologico-Politicus*
appeared in 1670 he said to Aubrey that Spinoza
"has cut through me a bar's length, for I durst not
write so boldly." It would indeed be difficult to blame
a timid old gentleman for not courting martyrdom.
The blame for reservation belongs to the persecutor
more than to the persecuted. It is, I think, far more
remarkable that Hobbes spoke so frankly than that he
did not reveal his whole mind. What he actually did
was to use language which, though it caused general
antipathy, and had implications quite clear to the
qualified reader, would have been difficult to cite as
proofs of punishable opinions in a legal indictment.
Every one is agreed to admire the admirable candour
and love of truth of Spinoza. Yet I think that the
meaning attached by Spinoza to the word "God" is
quite as unlike the ordinary meaning of theologians as
the meaning attached to it by Hobbes. Both have
defined their meaning quite frankly. If I say that an
object is white and add openly that by white I mean
what most people call black, I cannot be accused of
deception, though I may be taking advantage of the

verbal ambiguity which more or less binds the hands
of my enemies.   It might be pleasanter to drop all
disguise, but I am simply playing the game on the
terms which they themselves have chosen.   I do not,
indeed, feel certain that Hobbes admitted even to
himself the true nature of his position.   He may have
retained some of the horror for "atheism" in which
he had been educated and thrown dust in his own
eyes as well as in other people's.   My chief reason for
doubting is that, as we shall presently see, he relies, in
his political writings, upon certain doctrines as to
"the laws of God," which are apparently essential to
his argument, and which could hardly be used by one
to whom the words meant nothing.   It is true that
they do not in any case mean very much ; still it is
possible that Hobbes retained certain prepossessions
which, as it seems to me, were really incompatible
with his first principles.

3. *Determinism.*

I must now speak of Hobbes's position in regard to
the free-will controversy.

To mention the topic is enough to give the alarm
to all readers who are not in love with metaphysical
hair-splitting for its own sake.   It has become the
type of fruitless controversy.   Milton, in a familiar
passage, intimated that the argument was only suitable
to beings who had an indefinite amount of time on
their hands and to whom any distraction would be
agreeable.   At times, indeed, the popular mind is
startled by some supposed consequence of "determinism."   It is supposed to imply the existence of a

Fate which forces people, whether they like it or not, to commit so many murders in proportion to their population, or forces a sober person to take to drink because his grandfather was a drunkard. I am not about to argue the question, nor to follow in detail the brisk controversy between Hobbes and Bramhall. It will be enough to indicate briefly the position taken by Hobbes in regard to the contemporary phase of a perennial discussion. Milton's view was no doubt natural in the days of the Synod of Dort and the Westminster Assembly. The controversies between Catholics and Protestants necessarily involved conflicts over the free-will problem. In the Catholic doctrine the church is the appointed guardian of morality, conceived as a system of divine laws. The sacraments supply the means by which men may obtain grace to obey the law and receive forgiveness for transgressions. The whole system supposes that men have "free-will" and acquire "merit." They can either obey or disobey the law, and therefore they can deserve reward or punishment. The Protestant revolt against the authority of the Church led to the assertion of principles which when logically developed struck at the root of the whole system. A man can acquire no "merit," that is, no claim upon his Creator, for his obedience to the law. God, it must be supposed, approves a man for what he is, not for what he has done. One man may forgive another for an injury when compensation has been made. But the divine forgiveness can only mean that the will to do wrong is destroyed. Salvation must be gained, not by giving satisfaction for wrongs, but by the conformity of the man's nature to the divine order. The sinner must change his heart, not balance his accounts with his creditor. To the Protestant, therefore, the vital point became regeneration or conversion, and the sacraments have at most a secondary importance. But it then becomes difficult to admit "free-will." Man clearly cannot make himself. He cannot even contribute to the work of divine grace; for to allow him a share in the process is to admit some claim to "merit." Conversion, therefore, must be supernatural and the man merely passive.

While the Catholic divines were elaborating systems of casuistry and turning morality into a code of laws analogous to human legislation, the Protestants were endeavouring to form theories as to the action of divine grace upon the human heart. They discussed the "Five Articles" at the Synod of Dort, laid down dogmas as to predestination, election, the atonement, the corruption of human nature and its various consequences. The metaphysical controversy was continued with attempts to accept compromises with the old systems, and to find a sanction for every dogma in the Bible, regarded as a supernatural act of parliament, of which every word was divinely inspired. The discussion, instead of tending to unity, seemed to be only producing a ramification into diverging sects and conflicting dogmatisms. It might be shrewdly suspected that the reasoners were getting out of their depth, and it was clear that they were reaching some shocking results. When free-will has disappeared, it seems hard that a sinner should be tortured endlessly for doing what he was predestined to do. But how is the difficulty to be met? A century later Jonathan Edwards was led by his stern Calvinism to write one

of the acutest of all treatises upon free-will, and to
expound the doctrine of "determinism," or, as it was
called, "philosophical necessity." For the present,
the discussion was mixed up with heterogeneous elements, derived from the traditional dogmas. Hobbes,
though he cared little for theological dogmas, was
interested in the metaphysical part of the controversy.
He is very little given to quote authorities; but in his
discussion with Bramhall, he claims to be supported
on one essential point by Luther, Calvin, the Synod
of Dort, and other Protestant authorities. "All the
famous doctors of the Reformed Churches," he says,
"and with them St. Augustine, are of the same opinion."
The problem was in the air.

In England, Calvinism was going out of fashion.
The rationalist, disgusted by endless and fruitless
controversy, hoped that unity might be reached by
confining the creed to those points (if any) upon which
all Christians, or perhaps all religions, were agreed.
The metaphysical subtleties might be left to amuse
professors in their studies. The Anglican divines had
accepted Calvinism during the heat of their controversy with Rome. They were now opposing Calvinism
on one side as much as Rome on the other. "What
do the Arminians hold? All the best preferments in
England," was the famous quibble which marked the
changed attitude. The Church of England, claiming
to be the legitimate continuation of the mediæval
church, inherited the old theories as to the claims and
functions of the priesthood, which necessarily involved
a doctrine of free-will and a rejection of the Calvinism
which had for a time found acceptance. Bramhall was
a man of great vigour, who has been recently called by

a competent critic, "one of the ablest champions" of
the Church of England. He represented one special
antipathy of his opponent. Hobbes was never tired
of denouncing the "jargon" of the schoolmen, and
regarded their doctrines as the great obstacle in the
way of all intellectual progress. At the universities,
however, the schoolmen were still held in honour and
supplied the weapons for theological controversy.
Bramhall had sufficient training in the art to wield
their writings with familiarity and no little skill of
fence. When Hobbes speaks irreverently of these
authorities, Bramhall seems to be as much astonished
as disgusted. It seems as if he were quite unaware
that a revolt against the whole system had long been
in progress. He had obviously taken no interest in
the scientific movement represented by Bacon or
Hobbes. "It troubles him to see a scholar who hath
been long admitted into the innermost closet of nature
and seen the hidden secrets of more subtle learning,
so far forget himself as to style school learning no
better than a plain jargon, that is, a senseless gibberish
or a fustian language like the chattering noise of
sabots." Hobbes, he thinks, objects to scholastic distinctions, because a sore eye is offended by the sight
of the sun. Are all terms of art to be given up ? Is
the moral philosopher to "quit his means and extremes
. . ., his liberty of contradiction and contrariety ? "
Must the "natural philosopher give over his intentional
species . . . his receptive and eductive power of the
matter, his qualities *infusæ* or *influxæ, symbolæ* or *dis-
symbolæ,* his temperament *ad pondus* and *ad justitiam,*
. . . his sympathies and antipathies, his *antiperistasis,*
etc. ? Are the astrologer and the geographer to leave

their *apogœum* and *perigœum*, their arctic and antarctic
poles, their equator, zodiac, zenith, meridian, horizon,
zones, etc. ?" Hobbes will find that such things are
necessary in every art. Let him go on shipboard and
the mariners will not leave their *starboard* and *larboard*
because he accounts it gibberish. Hobbes is quite
ready to part with some of these words. Terms, he
thinks, should be thrown away when they cannot be
understood, and, when they can, should be used rightly.
The astrologer (unless the bishop means astronomer [1])
had better throw away his whole trade; but to the
astronomer "equator," "zodiac," and so forth, are as
useful as saw or hatchet to a carpenter. The "metaphysician" should quit both his terms and his profession,
and the divine use only such words as the hearer can
understand.

Bramhall therefore takes the airs of a philosophical
expert dealing with a coarse ignoramus. He may be
compared to a profound Hegelian lecturing a disciple
of J. S. Mill or Mr. Herbert Spencer. The scholastic
terminology appears obscure to Hobbes only because
the subject-matter is difficult and the listener stupid.
We do not now despise each other so heartily or express
our contempt so frankly. Bramhall claims the victory
with a confidence which is shared by his last editor,
who only regrets that he should not have met with an
antagonist "more worthy of him," and should have
wasted time in replying to "peevish and feeble
crotchets." I fancy that Bramhall is better remembered as Hobbes's opponent than Hobbes as Bramhall's;

[1] Bramhall had some belief in astrology. "All judicious
astronomers hold that the stars 'incline' though they do not
'necessitate' the will."

but they represent modes of thought so different, that it is easy to understand how each should be triumphant in the eyes of his own side.

Hobbes's main purpose is obvious. He aspires to apply scientific methods to what we now call psychological and sociological problems. This leads him, like many of his successors, to deny altogether the possibility of "free-will." Free-will, as he understands it, means the presence of an essentially arbitrary factor in human conduct. If we knew the whole character of a man and all the motives that act upon him, we should still, if free-will be a reality, be unable to predict his action. Everything else being the same, his choice is indeterminate. No one, of course, supposes his choice to be absolutely arbitrary; but, so far as the arbitrary element remains, scientific certainty is impossible. Science, according to Hobbes, means the deduction of effects from causes. Free-will supposes the so-called chain to be broken. Given the cause, the effect may be this or that. If this be really implied in the conception of free-will, it is obvious that if it does not destroy the possibility, it limits the field of moral science. Hobbes's whole doctrine is radically opposed to this theory. Man, he has told us, is moved by "appetites" and "aversions." On one side these appetites are literally "motions" in the physical organism : reactions set up by contact with outside things, following as necessarily as the motion of the hands of the clock follows from the descent of the weight. On the other side they appear to us as phantasms—as hopes of good and fears of evil; good being the same as the pleasurable, and evil as the painful. When we have alternating and conflicting hopes

and fears, we call the process "deliberation." The
resultant which determines the action is the last
appetite, or, as we call it, the will. The "passions,"
appetites, aversions, hopes, and fears do not, he says,
proceed from, they *are* the will. In his discussion with
Bramhall, Hobbes does not lay stress upon the physical
aspect. We know, he says, by reflecting on ourselves,
that "deliberation or choice" means simply considering
the good and evil consequences of our actions. Reflection will also convince us that nothing can begin
without a cause. Everything is caused : our actions
are caused by our expectations of good and evil, or
(which is identical) of pleasure and pain. Whether
we take it physiologically or psychologically, all conduct is determined, or, as he calls it, "necessary."
Freedom has still a precise meaning. It means the
"absence of all impediments to action that are not
contained in the nature of the agent." Thus defined,
freedom is compatible with "necessitation." I am free
when my action is necessitated by my own desires,
not by external conditions. I am not free to walk out
when the door is locked ; I am free when it is open.
But I am "necessitated to use my freedom by the
desire which causes me to walk out or not to walk
out"; only in this case the necessity is in my own
nature, not in the surroundings. Freedom, therefore,
as he constantly insists, means freedom to *do* what I
will; but freedom to *will* what I will is nonsense. A
man, in his illustration, may be free to eat if there is
no obstacle between him and his food. But he is not
free to have or not to have an appetite for his food.
That is settled by his organism. His will is the
appetite. The "freedom" of the will, understood as

denying causation, is an illusion. When we do not know the causes of volition, we assume that it is uncaused. Chance usually means our ignorance. Everything, he infers, is necessary. He ought rather, I think, to have argued that "necessary," like "probable," "possible," and so forth, really refers to our knowledge, and means no more than "certain." His use of the word seems to imply that besides the man and his circumstances, there is an external fate which coerces him.

So far, Hobbes is saying what has been said by later "determinists." Bramhall calls him the "ringleader of a new sect, or rather the first nominal Christian who has raised from its grave the 'sleeping ghost' of the Stoics' fate." Hobbes, if Bramhall is correct, may be credited with giving the purely scientific version of the doctrine more or less implied in the Calvinist theology. To Bramhall it naturally appears monstrous and unintelligible. He holds it to be as clear that "there are free actions which proceed merely from election without any outward necessitation" as that there is a sun in the heavens. That is the usual appeal to our consciousness of free-will. Hobbes, however, might accept the phrase, if amended, by the admission that there is "inward necessitation." They agree that voluntary action implies "deliberation." Hobbes considers that deliberation is as much determined or necessitated as any other natural process. Bramhall replies by one of the distinctions which to Hobbes were meaningless "jargon." The "motives" and "passions," he says, only move the will morally; they do not determine it naturally. Moral determination, according to Hobbes, is still determination. The

will, says Bramhall, hath a free dominion over itself;
she is the mistress of human actions; the understanding
is her trusty counsellor which she can consult or not
as she pleases. Bramhall talks, says Hobbes, as if the
will and the other faculties "were men or spirits in
men's bellies." It is the man and not the will who
decides. In this case Hobbes hits the mark. Bramhall seems to accept a kind of psychological mythology
in which abstractions like "the will" are personified,
and logical distinctions made to imply different
faculties in the concrete individual. Freedom no
doubt is a rational concept, for it does not imply contradiction. But it does not follow that because a
thing can be rightly described by an indeterminate
phrase, a concrete indeterminate thing can exist. I
will not, however, go into the argument. Bramhall, I
take it, cannot confute the theory that conduct is
caused, because there are no arguments by which it
can be confuted. It is consistent in itself. Whether
it can be proved or whether it is opposed to our
immediate consciousness are other questions which I
leave to those who are amused by them. Neither
need I speak of other arguments, which fill a large
space in the dispute, such as the argument from texts:
whether the famous passage in the Epistle to the
Romans denies free-will; or the question to the
paralytic person, "wilt thou be clean," implies that he
had free-will. Nor will I speak of the puzzles about
reconciling the divine prescience to "indeterminism";
or the difference between admitting that the Creator
permitted sin, and admitting that he caused it. The
arguments are familiar, and to Hobbes, Bramhall
seems to be constantly evading them by verbal dis-

tinctions. It is a fight between a man of science looking at the facts, and a skilful dialectician dodging them
under shelter of irrelevant concepts.

The horror felt for determinism is due to what
Hobbes calls "certain inconveniences" supposed to be
its consequences. For that reason Hobbes wished, he
says, to keep discussion private. A sinner might
excuse himself—however illogically—by saying that
his sin was predetermined. He did not want a
murderer to say, "Mr. Hobbes tells me that I couldn't
help it."

Now a rational theory of determinism may be, as I
think that it is, free from that objection. But Hobbes's
version leads to consequences which are startling to
the moralist and significant of his general attitude.
Bramhall, as his opponents hold, confuses determinism
with fatalism. He therefore argues that necessity
makes laws unjust, and all advice, praise, blame, books,
doctors, and tutors absurd. If the future is determined
by "unalterable necessity, whether we be idle or
industrious, why do we labour"? The answer is of
course obvious. The end is not determined irrespectively of the means. To say, "If I shall live till to-
morrow, I shall live though I run myself through with
a sword to-day," is absurd; for if I am fated to live
till to-morrow, I am also fated not to run myself
through to-day. It is not absurd to make a law
against crime, for the law alters the conditions, by
affecting the will. A man, it may be, cannot refrain
from murder when there is no law, but can when he
knows he is to be hanged for it. Murderers, says
Hobbes, are killed because they are noxious, not
because they are "not necessitated." Hobbes, that is,

accepts the purely deterrent theory of criminal law.
You are not hanged for stealing sheep, as the judge
said, but hanged in order that sheep may not be
stolen. Bramhall, he says, "takes punishment for a
kind of revenge." Hobbes, on the other hand, denies
that any good man will afflict another, except to reform
the will of the criminal or other men. "Nor can I
understand, having only human ideas, that that
punishment which neither intendeth the correction of
the offender nor the correction of others can proceed
from God ?" Hobbes, I take it, would in this be
approved by all rational law reformers. Punishment
is justifiable so far only as it tends to diminish crime,
and not because it gratifies a desire for vengeance which
prompts the infliction of superfluous suffering. Most
people, however, feel that his statement is insufficient.
We have a right to destroy "all that is noxious," says
Hobbes, "both beasts and men." We kill the murderer
as we kill the wolf ; and we kill the wolf "justly when
we do it in order to our own preservation." The
theory seems to omit an essential element in the case.
When we say that punishment should be "just," do we
not imply that there is some essential difference between
killing a wolf and hanging a murderer ? But Hobbes
is forced by his logic to take up one very questionable
position. Bramhall asks him what, upon his theory, is
the meaning of praise and blame ? If all actions be
necessary why are they praiseworthy or blameworthy ?
We blame people, says Hobbes, "because they please
us not." Blaming means the saying that a thing is
imperfect. A man is a fool or a knave even if he
cannot help it When it was said that Cato was
good by nature, *et quia aliter esse non potuit*, he surely

received very high praise. If necessity does not make
praise meaningless, why, asks Bramhall, do we not
praise fire for burning ? Men are the tennis-balls of
destiny, and are good and bad only as a ball is good
or bad. Hobbes replies that we do blame fire or
poison as much as we do men. We do not seek to be
revenged on them, "because we cannot make them ask
forgiveness, as we would make men to do when they
hurt us." The blame is the same in both, "but the
malice of man is only against man."

When Hobbes was pressed by a *reductio ad absurdum*
he generally had the courage to swallow the absurdity.
In this case his logic had put him in an awkward
place. Accepting his materialism and his thoroughgoing egoism, two men in opposition appear to us
simply as two tennis-balls coming into collision. The
man, no doubt, might be more consistently mischievous
than the ball, as he is supposed to be malicious. The
ball might sometimes give an impulse in the right
direction, while the wicked man will always aim at
doing injury. Still,so long as a man considers his own
feelings exclusively, the difference between blaming a
poison and blaming the poisoner seems to be one of
degree rather than of kind. The determinist may hold
that Hobbes's error lay, not in assuming that human
motives act regularly, but in failing to take into
account the man behind the thing, and those emotions
of love and hatred which imply sympathy and a direct
interest in the happiness or sorrow of others. The
difficulty comes out when he is arguing the question of
divine justice. Of God, according to Hobbes, we really
know nothing, except that He is omnipotent. It is,
then, only from that attribute that we can derive His

justice. Beasts are subject to death and torment; yet
"they cannot sin." It was God's will it should be so.
"Power irresistible justifieth all actions, really and properly, in whomsoever it be found." It is, he adds, to
be found in God only. "God cannot sin because his
doing a thing makes it just and consequently no sin;
and because whatsoever can sin is subject to another's
law, which God is not; and therefore it is blasphemy
to say God can sin." Hobbes, it would seem, would
have been more consistent if he had left out "justice"
altogether. His God—the creator of the physical universe—is the author of what the man of science calls "the
laws of nature." But they are simply the mechanical
laws. It is not "just" that weights should balance each
other when they are proportioned in a certain way to
the length of the arms of a lever; it is simply a fact.
Morality has nothing to do one way or the other with
the motions of the planets or the "laws of gravitation."
The physical system of the universe is morally neutral.
Morality can only begin with the conscious and sentient
being. The assumption, however, that a "law of
nature" means the same in both cases becomes very
important in Hobbes's theory of the State, where we
shall meet it again.

Meanwhile it may be remarked for the old gentleman's credit that he is shocked by one inference drawn
by others. Bramhall has argued from "eternal tor-
ments": their existence proves liberty. "To take away
liberty hazards heaven but undoubtedly it leaves no
hell." Some people might consider that consequence
to be a partial compensation. Bramhall, however, has
no doubt about hell; and the Calvinists, though they
took away liberty, were quite convinced that the

eternal torment of sinners was just. Hobbes was so
far with them that he was bound to admit the justice
of any actually existing arrangement, but he refuses
to admit the existence of hell. Though God may
"afflict a man, and not for sin, without injustice, shall
we think him so cruel as to afflict a man, and not for
sin, with extreme and endless torment? Is it not
cruelty? No more than to do the same for sin, when
he that so doeth might without trouble have kept him
from sinning." He asks, however, where the Scriptures say that "a second death is an endless life? Or
do the doctors say it? Then perhaps they do but say
so and for reasons best known to themselves." "It
seemeth hard to say," he observes elsewhere, "that God,
who is the father of mercies, that doth in heaven and
earth all that he will, that hath the hearts of all men in
his disposing, that worketh in men both to do and to
will . . . should punish men's transgressions without any
end of time and with all the extremity of torture that
men can imagine and more." Hobbes managed to
reconcile his theory to the orthodox view in a rather
singular fashion. But modern divines will not quarrel
with him for declining to believe in the old doctrine of
damnation.

One other remark must be added. Hobbes is not
content with resolving the divine justice into power.
Human justice is equally the creature of power.
Natural goodness differs, he says, from moral. A
horse has natural goodness if he is strong and gentle
and so forth; and if there were no laws, there would
be as much "moral good" in a horse as in a man. It
is the law which makes the difference. Law-makers
may err; but from obedience to the law, whether

made in error or not, proceeds "moral praise." Since
our notions of good and bad are relative and mean
simply what pleases or displeases us, we can only get a
common rule by subjection to the law. "All the real
good, which we call honest and morally virtuous, is
that which is not repugnant to the law, civil or natural;
for the law is all the right reason we have, and . . .
is the infallible rule of moral goodness." Our fallibility
compels us to "set up a sovereign governor" and
agree that his law shall be to us in the place of right
reason. He illustrates this principle from card-
playing. When men have turned up trumps, "their
morality consisteth in not renouncing," that is, in
observing the rules of the game; and so "in civil
conversation our morality is all contained in not dis-
obeying of the laws."

This doctrine—not at first sight very satisfactory—
will be more intelligible when we have considered the
Leviathan.

CHAPTER IV.

THE STATE [1]

1. *Contemporary Controversies*

WE come now to the third part of Hobbes's philosophy. He is to base a science of politics upon the doctrines already expounded. We become aware that there is a certain breach of continuity. To understand his line of thought, it is necessary to take note both of the problems in which he was specially interested, and the form into which the arguments had been moulded by previous thinkers. He applies to the questions of the day certain conceptions already current in political theory, though he uses them in such a way as materially to alter their significance.

Hobbes's theory in the first place involves the acceptance of a so-called "Law of Nature." "Nature," as we know, is a word contrived in order to introduce as many equivocations as possible into all the theories, political, legal, artistic, or literary, into which it enters.

[1] Hobbes's political theory is given in three books: the *De Corpore Politico*, which was the second part of his first treatise, and is reprinted in the fourth volume of the English works; the *De Cive*, which is in the Latin works, vol. iii., and an English translation of which, by Hobbes himself, forms the second volume of the English works; and the *Leviathan*, which forms the third volume of the English works.

The "Law of Nature," as writers upon jurisprudence tell us, was invented by Roman lawyers with the help of Stoic philosophers. The lawyers, having to deal with the legal systems of the numerous races which came into contact with Rome, were led to recognise a certain body of laws common to all. Such law came to be considered as laid down by Nature. It was a product of the human nature common to Greeks and Romans, and not affected by the special modifications by which Romans are distinguished from Greeks. It belonged to the genus man, not to the species nation. The philosopher, meanwhile, took the Law of Nature to be law imposed by the divine author of nature, discoverable by right reason, and therefore common to all reasoning beings. The law in either case is "natural" because universally valid. But this may cover two diverging conceptions. To the man of science "nature" means everything actually existing. One quality cannot be more "natural" than another, though it may be more widely diffused. A scientific investigator of jurisprudence would inquire what systems of law prevail in different countries, and would seek to discover the causes of uniformity or difference. The inquirer is so far simply concerned with the question of fact, and to him the exceptional is just as much a natural product as the normal legislation. The scientific point of view is that from which one might expect Hobbes to treat the question. He accepts, however, the Law of Nature in another sense. It meant an ideal, not an actual law, and tells us what ought to be, not what is. There may of course be a presumption that a law (if there is such law) which is universally accepted is also dictated by

reason ; or a state may be so happily constituted that
the perception that a law is reasonable may involve
its acceptance in the actual system. But in any case
the Law of Nature is supposed to be the type to which
the actual law should be made to conform, and therefore implies a contrast and occasional conflict between
the two systems.

Hobbes's view implies another distinction. Every
one admits that laws may rightly vary according
to circumstances within certain limits. There are
laws, we may say, which it is right to obey because
they are the law, and others which are the law because
it is right to obey them. In England the law of the
road tells carriages to keep to the left, and in France
to keep to the right. We clearly ought to obey each
rule in its own country. But there are other cases.
In some countries the law permits or enforces rules of
marriage which in other countries are held to be
immoral and revolting. Is it true in this case also
that each law is right in its own country, or is one set
of laws to be condemned as contrary to the Law of
Nature ? Given the Law of Nature, that is, how are
we to decide what sphere of discretion is to be left to
the legislator ? Can he deal with the most vital as well
as the most trivial relations, or how is his proper sphere
of authority to be defined ? Where does " positive "
law begin and natural law end ? This involves the
problem, How far does the power of the legislature
extend ?—or, What is the relation between the sovereign
and the subject. That was a problem which had not
been discussed in the classical philosophy. Man as a
" political animal " was so identified with the State
that citizenship was an essential part of him. Different

forms of government might be compared, but the individual could not be conceived as existing independently of the State. To Hobbes the State had become an "artificial" construction, and therefore its relation to the units of which it was constructed had to be settled and was vitally important.

The theory of sovereignty had become interesting when there were rival claimants to sovereignty. The Christian Church, beginning as a voluntary association outside the State, and appealing to men in their individual capacity, had become a gigantic organisation with an elaborate constitution and legal system. It had come into collision, alliance, and rivalry with the empire. According to the accepted theory, both powers had legitimate claims to allegiance. Pope and emperor were compared to the sun and moon, though it might be disputed which was the sun and which was the moon, or whether they were not rather two independent luminaries. In the great controversies which arose, the Church had an obvious advantage. It derived its authority from direct revelation. It represented on earth the supreme Being, and was entrusted by him with power to enforce the moral laws which coincide with the Law of Nature. As the empire could claim no special revelation, the advocates of its claims had to find some independent support for them in the Law of Nature. To the question, then, Whence is derived the obligation to obey the State, or rather the ruler? there was but one obvious answer. "All obligation," says Hobbes, "derives from contract" It is part of the Law of Nature that man should observe compacts. If therefore the relation between sovereign and subject depends upon a compact, there is a sufficient obligation to obedience though the ruler has not a special commission from God. It could not, it is true, be proved that such a compact had ever been made, nor that, if made in one generation, it would be binding on the next, nor was it possible to say what were the exact terms of the supposed compact. But such cavils were trifles. They could be met by saying that there was an "implicit" contract, and that it, no doubt, prescribed reasonable terms. This theory was gradually developed in the Middle Ages, and when Hobbes was a young man it had acquired especial currency from the great book in which Grotius had adopted it, when applying the Law of Nature to regulate the ethics of peace and war.[1]

This set of conceptions gives Hobbes's starting-point, though in his hands the Law of Nature and the social compact received a peculiar development or, indeed, seemed to be turned inside out. He applied them to the great controversies in which he and his contemporaries were specially interested. The complicated struggles of the Reformation period had raised issues which were still undecided. Church and State, whatever the theory of their relations, were so closely connected as to form parts of one organism, and a separation of them, such as is contemplated by modern speculation, was unthinkable. If the two bodies had conflicting claims, they were also recipro-

---

[1] A very remarkable book, the *Politics* of Johannes Althusius (1557-1636), that appeared in 1603, anticipated much that Hobbes afterwards said, and played a considerable part in the evolution of the theory of "Naturrecht." Professor Gierke's most learned and interesting book upon Althusius gives a full account of his doctrine and of his relation to Hobbes among many others.

M

cally necessary. Their systems of legislation were not independent, but interpenetrating. Each implied the other, and the State was bound to suppress heresy, as the Church to condemn rebellion. The disruption of the old system implied both civil and foreign war. The lines of cleavage ran through both Church and State, and in each fragment the ecclesiastical and secular system had to readjust their relations. When in England Henry VIII. renounced the authority of the pope, he had to become a bit of a pope himself. In Scotland the Church, though it might suppose that it had returned to primitive purity, could not be expected for that reason to relinquish its claims to authority over the laity. In the famous "Monarcho-machist" controversy, Jesuits agreed with Scottish Protestants and French Huguenots in defending tyrannicide. They had a common interest in limiting the claims of the secular power. Jacques Clément and Ravaillac gave a pointed application in France to the Jesuit doctrine; and the Scots had to make a case against Queen Mary. Meanwhile the claims of the Catholic Church were the cause or the pretext of the warfare which culminated in the Spanish Armada. The patriotic Englishman regarded the pope as the instigator or accomplice of the assailants of our national independence. Persecution of priests seemed to be necessary, even if cruel, when priests were agents of the power which supported hostile fleets and inspired murderous conspiracies. Throughout the seventeenth century the protestant Englishman suffered from "papacy" on the brain, and his fear flashed into panic for the last time when Hobbes was dying. During his youth the keenest controversy had been raging over the claims of the papacy. James I. himself and his most learned divines, such as Andrewes and Donne, were arguing against the great Catholic divines, Suárez and Bellarmine. The controversy turned especially upon the imposition of the oath renouncing the doctrine of the right of the pope to depose kings. To that right was opposed the "divine right of kings": thereby being meant, not that kings had a "right divine to govern wrong," but that the king's right was as directly derived from Heaven as the rights of the Church.

Hobbes, as we shall see, was deeply impressed by these problems. The power of the Catholic Church to enforce its old claims was rapidly disappearing; but men are often most interested in discussing the means of escaping the dangers of the day before yesterday. While Hobbes was elaborating his system, great political issues seemed to turn upon the relation between the spiritual and secular authority. Meanwhile the purely political were inextricably mixed up with ecclesiastical questions. James's formula, "no bishop, no king," expressed the fact. The Church of England was in the closest alliance with the royal authority; "passive obedience" to the king became almost an essential doctrine, even with liberal Anglican divines; and the rebellion was the outcome of the discontent in both spheres. In England the claim of parliament to a share of power came first, but the power was to be applied on behalf of religious Puritanism. In Scotland the Church question was most prominent; but the Church, in the rule of which, as James complained, Tom, Dick, and Harry had claimed to have a voice, also represented the aspirations of the nation. The political problem was equally important, whatever might be the motives for demanding political power. The question in England was whether the ancient parliamentary institutions were to be preserved and developed, or to be allowed to fall into decay as in other European countries where the State was being organised on different lines. In later days, writers who held the British constitution to be an embodiment of perfect wisdom, naturally venerated the Hampdens and Eliots as representatives of the ultimately victorious, and therefore rightful cause.

As Hobbes altogether condemned their principles, we must remind ourselves how things appeared at the time. To men who desired a vigorous national government—which is surely a very reasonable desire —the claims of the parliamentary party appeared to be a hopeless obstacle. All men admitted that the king was to have the fullest authority over the national policy ; he might make war or peace without consulting anybody ; and, if he could make it at his own expense, parliament had no ground for interference. The only thing which it could do was to refuse money if he wanted it for a policy which it disliked. It was as if the crew of a ship of war gave the command unreservedly to the captain, but, if they disliked the direction in which he was steering, showed disapproval by turning off the steam. That obviously would be a clumsy method. Parliament did not superintend or give general directions, but could throw the whole system out of gear when it pleased. We know, of course, how the struggle resulted in the supremacy of parliament, and of that party organisation which enabled it to act as a unit, and to regulate the whole national policy with a certain continuity of purpose. In Hobbes's time not only could such a system, as historians agree, occur to no one, but if it had occurred it would have been impracticable. To be efficient it required, not merely an exposition of principles, but the development of a mutual understanding between the different classes, which was not less essential because not expressed in any legal document. The art of parliamentary government has to be learnt by practice.

Another remark is now pretty obvious. The British people managed to work out a system which had, as we all believe, very great advantages and may justify some of the old panegyrics. Men could speak more freely—if not always more wisely—in England than elsewhere, and individual energy developed with many most admirable, if with some not quite admirable consequences. But the success was won at a cost. The central authority of the State was paralysed; and many observers may admit that, in securing liberty at the price of general clumsiness and inefficiency of all the central administrative functions, the cost has been considerable. It is desirable to remember this point when we come to Hobbes's special theories. To him the demands of the parliamentary party appeared to imply a hopeless disorganisation of the political machinery. His political writings, though professing to be a piece of abstract logic, are also essentially aimed at answering these questions. The vital problem involved was, as he thought, What is sovereignty and who should be sovereign? The State, on one side, was struggling with the Church—whether the Church of Rome or the Church of Scotland—and, on

the other hand, the supreme power was claimed for
king alone, for parliament alone, and for some com≈
bination of the two. What will a scientific analysis
enable us to say as to the general nature of the
supreme power and as to the best constitution of a
body politic? The country, as he says, for some years
before the civil war, "was boiling over with questions
concerning the rights of dominion and the obedience
due from subjects": a state of things which "ripened
and plucked" from him the third part of his philosophy before the other parts were ready.

2. *The Social Contract.*

Hobbes's political theories are expounded in the
De Corpore Politico (the little treatise of 1640), the *De
Cive,* and the *Leviathan.* The title of the last of these
works is suggested by certain words in the Book of
Job: "*Non est potestas super terram quæ comparetur ei.*"
They are printed at the head of the quaint allegorical
title-page, where a composite giant, his body made of
human beings, holds the sword in one and a crosier in
the other hand, while beneath him is a wide country
with a town, a fort, and a church in the foreground, and
below it are various symbols of temporal and spiritual
power. The great Leviathan, he tells us, is that
mortal god to which we owe, under the immortal God,
our peace and defence. But he is also a machine. We
are to take him to pieces in imagination, as we actually
take to pieces a watch to understand its construction. We have already seen the statement of Hobbes's
method. It is impossible to deduce the properties of
this complex mechanism by the synthetical method;

but by analysing the observed "motions of the mind" we can discover its essential principles. Justice, he says, means giving to each man his own. How does a man come to have an "own"? Because community of goods breeds contention, while reason prescribes peace. From the regulation of the "concupiscible" nature by the "rational" arises the system of moral and civil laws embodied in the great Leviathan. We have to examine this process in detail. Men have, as we have seen, "a perpetual and restless desire of power after power" In the next place, men are naturally equal. The weakest in body, at any rate, may kill the strongest, and there is a still greater equality in mind. This doctrine of natural equality he tries to establish by rather quaint arguments. "Every man," he says, "thinks himself as wise, though not as witty or learned as his neighbours. What better proof can there be of equality of distribution than that every man is contented with his share?" That is hardly convincing; but what Hobbes means to say is, that no man has such a superiority over his fellows as would make him secure in the chaotic struggle of "the state of nature." When two men want the same thing, therefore, each will have a chance. Competition, diffidence (a distrust of each other), and glory (the desire, we may say, for prestige) are the three principal causes of quarrel. "The first maketh men invade for gain; the second for safety; the third for reputation." When there is no common power to overawe, there will be a "war of every man against every man." War, he explains, is not confined to actual fighting, but exists where there is a "known disposition thereto" and "no assurance to the contrary." So long as this state

continues, "there is no place for industry, because the
fruit thereof is uncertain," and (besides many other
wants) "no arts, no letters, no society, and which is
worst of all, continual fear and danger of violent
death; and the life of man solitary, poor, nasty,
brutish, and short." Do you object to this account of
man? Look at experience. Does not a man arm
himself when he is going a journey? Does he not
lock the chests in his own house, although he knows
that there are public officers to protect them? What
opinion does that imply of his fellow subjects or of
his servants? "Does he not as much accuse mankind
by his actions, as I do by my words?"

But was there ever such a "state of nature"? Not
perhaps over the whole world, though in America
many savages live in this nasty and brutish fashion.
If however, that were not so with particular men,
"yet in all times kings and persons of sovereign authority, because of their independency, are in continual
jealousies, and in the state and posture of gladiators;
having their weapons pointing and their eyes fixed on
one another—that is their forts, garrisons, and guns
upon the frontiers of their kingdoms—and continual
spies upon their neighbours." The argument is
certainly not obsolete, nor the remark which follows.
"Because they uphold thereby the industry of their
subjects, there does not follow from it that misery
which accompanies the liberty of particular men."
Now where every man is at war with every man, "the
notions of right and wrong, justice and injustice,have
no place. Where there is no common power there is
no law; where no law, no injustice. Force and fraud
are in war the two cardinal virtues." Justice and

injustice "relate to men in society, not in solitude."
In such a state of things, there can be "no *mine* and
thine distinct, but only that to be every man's that he
can get and for so long as he can keep it."

> ". . . the good old rule
> Sufficeth them, the simple plan,
> That they should take who have the power,
> And they should keep who can,"

as Wordsworth puts it. This is the "ill condition"
in which man is placed "by mere nature." There is a
possibility of his getting out of it, partly because some
passions, fear of death, desire of comfort, and hope of
securing it induce men to peace, and partly because
"reason suggesteth convenient articles of peace."

This is Hobbes's famous theory that the "state of
nature" is a state of war. It does not imply, he says,
that men are "evil by nature." The desires are not
themselves wicked, though at times they may cause
wicked actions. "Children grow peevish and do hurt
if you do not give them all they ask for; but they do
not become wicked till, being capable of reason, they
continue to do hurt." A wicked man is a child grown
strong and sturdy; and malice is a defect of reason at
the age when reasonable conduct is to be expected.
Nature provides the faculties but not the education.
The doctrine should be tested by its truth, not by its
pleasantness. Hobbes accepts in part the method of
Machiavelli, who clearly announced that he was concerned with what actually happened, not with what
ought to happen. To adopt that plan is to undertake
to tell unpleasant truths, and to tell unpleasant truths
is, according to most readers, to be "cynical." Hobbes

incurred the blame; but, at least, he was so far pursuing the truly scientific method. Up to this point, indeed, he was taking the line which would be followed by a modern inquirer into the history of institutions. Warfare is part of the struggle for existence out of which grow states and the whole organisation of civilised societies. A modern would maintain, like Hobbes, that, in admitting the part played by selfish force in the development of society, he does not assert the wickedness of human nature. He only asserts that the good impulses cannot acquire the desirable supremacy until a peaceful order has been established by the complex struggles and alliances of human beings, swayed by all their passions and ambitions. But, here we come upon an element in Hobbes's theory of which I have already spoken, namely, the Law of Nature. The "laws of human nature," in the scientific sense, expressing the way in which human beings actually behave, are identified with the Law of Nature as an ideal or divine law, which declares how men ought to behave. Hobbes professes to show that the sovereign has certain "rights" as well as certain powers; and, moreover, that those rights are far from being recognised in many countries and especially in England. He is not simply pointing out how it came to pass that Charles I. and his parliament had got into conflict, and thence inferring the best mode of settling the disputed points; but he desires to show that the "Law of Nature" decides the question of their conflicting rights. The "Nature" which prescribes the right cannot be identical with the "Nature" which gives the power and determines the facts.

Hobbes's next point, therefore, is to show what are the "Laws of Nature." Every man has a right, he says, to use his own power for his own preservation. A "Law of Nature" is a precept found out by reason, forbidding him to do the contrary : that is, to destroy himself or his means of self-preservation. Now, in the "state of nature" just described, every man has a right to everything—even to another man's body. He has a "right," that is, because nature makes self-preservation the sole aim of each man, even when it implies the destruction of others. But it is plain that, while this is the case, no man's life or happiness is secure. "Nature," therefore, orders men to get out of the "state of nature" as soon as they can. Hence we have the twofold principle. It is the "fundamental *law* of nature" that every man should "seek peace and follow it"; and the fundamental "*right* of nature" is that a man should defend himself by every means he can. Peace makes self-defence easy. It follows that a man should "lay down his right to all things" if other men will lay down theirs. This is identified by Hobbes with the "law of the Gospel": "*Whatsoever you require that others should do to you, that do ye to them*" or (which he takes to be equivalent); "*Quod tibi fieri non vis alteri ne feceris.*" A man may simply renounce or he may transfer a right. In either case, he is said to be "obliged" not to interfere with the exercise of a right by those to whom he has abandoned or granted it. It is his "duty" not to make his grant void by hindering men from using the right; and such hindrance is called "injustice." We thus have Hobbes's definitions of Obligation, Duty, and Justice. Injustice, he observes, is like an absurdity in logic. It is a contra-

diction of what you had voluntarily asserted that you
would do.

From these definitions, Hobbes proceeds to deduce
other "Laws of Nature," and finds no less than
nineteen. The third law (after those prescribing
peace and self-defence) is that men should keep their
"covenants." He afterwards deduces the duties
of gratitude, sociability, admission of equality—the
breach of which is pride—equity, and so forth. If, he
says, the "deduction" seems "too subtile," they may
all be regarded as corollaries from the "golden rule."
That rule, however, is itself deducible from the rule of
"self-preservation." We do good to others in order
that they may do good to us. "No man giveth," as
he says, by way of proving that gratitude is a virtue,
"but with intention of good to himself." . . . "Of
all voluntary acts, the object is to every man his own
good." That, one would rather have supposed, is a
reason for not being "grateful" to anybody. We
must interpret "gratitude" in the prospective sense—
with an eye to the favours to come. It is prudent to
pay your debts in order to keep up your credit. In
one case he seems to deviate a little from his egoism.
Justice means keeping covenants—obedience, that is,
to his "third law." A man who does a just action
from fear, as he remarks, is not therefore a just man;
his "will is not framed by the justice, but by the
apparent benefit of what he is to do. That which
gives to human actions the relish of justice is a certain
nobleness or gallantness of courage, rarely found, by
which a man scorns to be beholden for the contentment
of his life to fraud or breach of promise." He should
have held, it would seem, that the will is always

framed by the "apparent benefit." The inconsistency
(if there be one, for even this appears to be a case of
"glory") is explicable. Hobbes has to deduce all the
"Laws of Nature" from the law of self-preservation.
That, no doubt, may show the expediency of making
a "covenant" with your neighbours, and even the
expediency of generally keeping it. But it must also
be granted that there are occasions in which expediency
is in favour of breaking covenants. The just man, the
ordinary moralist would say, is a man who keeps his
word even to his own disadvantage. That, on the
strictest interpretation of Hobbes, is impossible. Nobody can do it. Justice, however, in the sense of
"covenant-keeping," is so essential a part of his system,
that he makes an implicit concession to a loftier tone
of morality, and admits that a man may love justice
for its own sake. This, however, seems to be an over-
sight. Hobbes is content to take for granted that
each man will profit by that which is favourable to
all, or that the desire for self-preservation will always
make for the preservation of society. The Law of
Nature, we see, is simply an application of the purely
egoistic law of self-preservation. It represents the
actual forces which (in Hobbes's view) mould and
regulate all human institutions. But in sanctioning
so respectable a virtue as "justice," it takes a certain
moral colouring, and may stand for the ideal Law of
Nature or Reason to which the actual order ought to
conform.

There is another reserve to be made : the laws of
nature are not properly laws. They are only "theorems
concerning what conduceth" to self-preservation. They
become laws proper when they are "delivered in the

Word of God"; and he proceeds in the *De Cive* to prove
them by a number of texts, and comes to the edifying
conclusion that the "Law of Nature" is the Law of
Christ. It is a theorem, for example, that to keep your
word tends to self-preservation. But law means the command of a rightful superior; and until such a command
has been given, it is not properly a "Law of Nature"
that you should keep your word. The laws are always
binding *in foro interno*: you are always bound to desire
that they should come into operation; but they are
not always binding *in foro externo*; that is, you are not
always bound to "put them in act." Self-preservation
is the fundamental law. But till other people keep
the laws, obedience to them does not tend to self-preservation. If you are peaceful and truthful when
other men are not, you will "procure your own certain
ruin, contrary to all the Laws of Nature." That
obviously will be the case in the "state of nature,"
where fraud and force are the cardinal virtues. There
is, no doubt, a truth in this contention. The moral
law, to become operative in fact, requires a certain
amount of reciprocity. Actual morality clearly depends upon the stage of social evolution. In a
primitive society where men have to defend themselves by the strong hand, we can hardly condemn
the man who accepts the standard methods. Achilles
would be a brutal ruffian to-day; but,when Troy was
besieged, he was a hero deserving admiration. He
was perhaps in the true line of development. The
chief of a savage tribe is, on the whole, preparing the
way for a peaceful order. Even in the present day
a philanthropist living in one of the regions where the
first-comer is ready to shoot him at sight might think

it right to carry a revolver in his pocket, and, if necessary, to anticipate the shooting. Moral rules become
useful in proportion as society perceives their value,
and is more or less inclined to adopt them in practice.
Otherwise, the man whose morality was of a higher type
would be thrown away or summarily stamped out.
Ought a man to be several generations in advance of
his time? That is a pretty problem which I do not
undertake to solve. In any case, Hobbes had a real
and important meaning. He saw, that is, that the
development of morality implies the growth of a
certain understanding between the individuals com-
posing the society, and that until this has been reached
ideal morality proper to a higher plane of thought is
impracticable if not undesirable. This leads to the
theory of the social contract—the mutual agreement
by which the great Leviathan is constructed.

The Law of Nature prescribes peace as a condition
of security. But the law is "contrary to our natural
passions," and "covenants without the sword are but
words and of no strength to secure a man at all." It
is therefore essential to create a common power to
keep men in awe. Such creatures as bees and ants
do, indeed, live at peace with each other and are
therefore called by Aristotle "political creatures."
Why cannot men do so? Because men compete and
have private aims different from the common good.
Men too can talk and therefore reason; they are
"most troublesome when most at ease," because they
then love to show their wisdom and control their
rulers. The great difference, however, is that their
agreement is "by covenant, which is artificial,"
whereas bees agree by "nature." By "artificial"

we must here understand what is made by reason.
Since men can live, for they do sometimes live, in
a "state of nature," a political society is not essential
to man as man. It is a product of his voluntary
action, and therefore implies a conscious deliberation.
The only way, then, in which the common power can
be erected and security established, is that men should
"confer all their power and strength upon one man
or one assembly of men." Then wills will be "reduced
into one will, and every man acknowledge himself to
be the author of whatsoever is done by the ruler so
constituted." "This is more than consent or concord;
it is a real unity of them all in one and the same
person, made by covenant of every man with every
man; in such manner as if every man should say
to every man : '*I authorise and give up my right of governing myself to this man, or this assembly of men, on this
condition that thou give up thy right to him, and authorise
all his actions in like manner.*'" The Leviathan, or mortal
God, is instituted by this covenant. He is the vital
principle of political association, and from it Hobbes
will proceed to deduce the whole of his doctrine.

Before considering its terms, one remark may be
made. It is sometimes asked whether the expounders
of the "social contract" in various forms meant to be
understood historically. Did they mean to assert that
at some remote period a number of men had held a
convention, like the American States, and signed
articles of association, to bind themselves and their
posterity? Occasionally they seem to be driven to
accept that position. Hobbes, however, can hardly
have entertained such a belief. He is as ready as
anybody to give an historical account of the origin

of actual constitutions. In his *Dialogue upon the
Common Law*, for example, he, like Montesquieu,
traces the origin of the British Constitution to the
forests of Germany, and the system once prevalent
among the "savage and heathen" Saxons. He re-
cognises in the *Leviathan* that governments may arise
from conquest or the development of the family as
well as by "institution," and endeavours to show that
the nature of sovereignty will be the same in whatever
way it may have originated. A contract, it always
has to be admitted, may be "implicit" (that is, may
really be no contract at all), and there can be no doubt
that, in point of fact, the social contract, if it exists,
must at the present day be of that kind. Nobody is
ever asked whether he will or will not agree to it.
Men, as members of a political society, accept a certain
relation to the sovereign, and unless they did so the
society would be dissolved. That such an understanding exists, and is a condition of the existence of
the State, would be enough for Hobbes, whatever the
origin of the understanding. As we shall presently
see, he would be more consistent, if not more edifying,
if he threw the contract overboard altogether.

We must look more clearly at the terms of the
hypothetical contract. The first point is that Hobbes's
version differs from the earlier forms in this, that it is
not a contract between the subject and the sovereign,
but between the subjects themselves. The sovereign
is created by it, but is not a party to it. This is
Hobbes's special and most significant contribution to
the theory. His reason is plain. Men in a state
of nature, that is, not acknowledging any common
authority, cannot make a contract collectively. They

N

are, in that case, simply a "multitude." His own
theory, he says in a note to the *De Cive*, depends upon
clearly understanding the different senses in which
this word may be used. A multitude means first a
multitude of men. Each has his own will and can
make compacts with his neighbours. There may be
as many compacts as there are men, or pairs of men,
but there is then no such thing as a common will or
a contract of the multitude considered as a unit.
This first becomes possible when they have each agreed
that the will of some one man or of a majority shall
be taken for the will of all. Then the multitude
becomes a "person," and is generally called a "people."
One man is a "natural person," and their common
representative is an "artificial person," or, as he puts
it, "bears the person of the people." It is, therefore,
impossible to take the social contract as made between
the sovereign and the subjects. Till they have become
an "artificial person" they cannot make a contract as
a whole. This social contract is presupposed in all
other contracts. It must be at the foundation of all
corporate action, and a compact between the sovereign
and the subjects would suppose the previous existence
of a unity which is only created by the contract itself.
In the "state of nature" men can promise but cannot
make a binding contract. A contract means an ex-
change of promises, and in a "state of nature" neither
party can depend upon the other keeping his word.
Obligation follows security. It seems rather difficult,
perhaps, to see how you can ever get out of the state
of nature, or why the agreement of each man to take
the sovereign will for his own is more likely to be
observed than any other agreement. Hobbes, how-

ever, assumes that this is possible; and when the
Leviathan has once been constructed, it embodies the
common will. The multitude becomes a person, and
law, natural and civil, becomes binding.

3. " *The Leviathan*."

We have thus got our sovereign. His will is the
will of all. He is under no obligation to his subjects,
but is the source of all obligation. The ultimate
justification of his existence, however, is still the desire
for self-preservation, and for peace as an essential
condition. Hence, indeed, arise the only limitations
to the power of the sovereign, which Hobbes admits.
Since I aim at my own security, I cannot lay down
the right of resisting men who would kill me, or even
men "who would inflict wounds or imprisonment."
I may indeed agree that you shall kill me, but I
cannot agree that I will not resist you. A criminal
may be properly put to death, for he has agreed
to the law; but he must be guarded on his way to
execution, for he has not bargained not to run
away. He adds another quaint exception. A man
may refuse to serve as a soldier, at least if he
can offer a substitute. "And," he adds, "there is
allowance to be made for natural timorousness, not
only to women, of whom no such dangerous duty is
expected, but also to men of feminine courage." (They
may have been born in 1588.) In such cases, it seems,
disobedience does not "frustrate the end for which
sovereignty was ordained." The principle applies to
the case of *de facto* government—when the sovereign
cannot defend me I need not obey him.

With these exceptions, the power of the sovereign is unlimited. The "mortal God" is omnipotent. The covenant once made is indefeasible. The parties to it cannot make a new covenant inconsistent with it. They cannot transfer their allegiance without the consent of the sovereign. Since there is no power of revising the covenant, it cannot be broken without injustice. Hobbes, we see, speaks of the sovereign as "representing" the subjects. But he does not "represent" them as a member of parliament represents his constituents, or as a delegate bound to carry out their wishes. He "represents" them in the sense that whatever he does is taken to be done by them. They are as responsible for all his actions as though he was their volition incorporated. It follows that his power can never be forfeited. The subjects have done whatever he has done, and in resisting him would be calling themselves to account. The social contract, considered as a covenant with the ruler, was alleged as a justification of rebellion. Hobbes inverts the argument. It can never be right to allege a "covenant" with the ruler, because that would justify rebellion. Since there is no common judge in such a case, this would mean an appeal to the power of the sword, and the power of the sword is what you have abandoned in covenanting. No individual again can dissent. If he does, he "may justly be destroyed" by the rest. If he consented to covenant, he implicitly consented to the covenant actually made. But, if not, he is left in the state of nature and may, therefore, "without injustice be destroyed by any man whatsoever."

The Leviathan, thus constituted, has therefore an

indefeasible title and is irresponsible. He is the
ultimate authority from whom all rights are derived.
The end of his institution is peace. A right to the end
implies a right to the means. The sovereign may do
whatever promotes peace. Since men's actions proceed
from their opinions, he may suppress the publication of
opinions tending in his opinion to disturb the peace.
Since contention arises from the clashing of rights, he
must determine men's rights; or, in other words, must
be the supreme legislator. The law means the command of the sovereign, and whatever he commands is
therefore law. He must, again, have the "right of judicature"; the right to hear and decide all controversies
arising out of the law. The sword of justice belongs
to him, and "the sword of justice must go with the
sword of war." The sovereign has to protect the
people against foreign enemies as well as to protect
each man against his neighbour. He must decide upon
war and peace; and when war is necessary must decide
what forces are necessary; and, further, must decide
how much money is required to pay for them. "The
command of the militia" (the military forces in general),
"without other institution, maketh him that hath it
sovereign; and, therefore, whosoever is made general
of an army, he that hath the sovereign power is always
generalissimo." Other powers, such as the appointment of ministers, the distribution of honours, and the
infliction of punishments obviously follow.

The Leviathan, thus invested with fullest power of
legislature, judicature, and military command, with
authority over opinion, and right to levy taxes,
appeared to Hobbes's contemporaries to be a terrible
portent. Charles I., trying to dispense with parlia-

ments, Cromwell ruling by armed force, Louis XIV.
declaring himself to be the State, might be taken as
avatars of the monster. Lovers of liberty of thought
or action were shocked by a doctrine fit only for the
graceless and abject courtiers of the Restoration. The
doctrine, however, must be considered on more general
grounds. Hobbes, in the first place, is not here arguing
for one form of government more than for another.
He prefers monarchy; but his special point is that in
every form, monarchic, aristocratic, or democratic, there
must be a "sovereign"—an ultimate, supreme and
single authority. Men, he says, admit the claim of a
popular State to "absolute dominion," but object to
the claim of a king, though he has the same power and
is not more likely, for reasons given, to abuse it. The
doctrine which he really opposes is that of a "mixed
government." As "some doctors" hold that there are
three souls in one man, others hold that there can be
more souls than one in a commonwealth. That is
virtually implied when they say that "the power of
levying money, which is the nutritive faculty," depends
on a "general assembly"; the "power of conduct and
command, which is the motive faculty, on one man; and
the power of making laws, which is the rational faculty,
on the accidental consent, not only of those two last, but
of a third": this is called "mixed monarchy." "In
truth it is not one independent commonwealth, but three
independent factions; nor one representative person
but three. In the Kingdom of God there may be
three persons independent without breach of unity in
God that reigneth; but where men reign that be subject to diversity of opinions, it cannot be so. And
therefore if the king bear the person of the people, the

general assembly bear the person of the people, and
another assembly bear the person of a part of the
people, they are not one person, nor one sovereign, but
three persons and three sovereigns." That is to say,
the political, like the animal organism, is essentially
a unit. So far as there is not somewhere a supreme
authority, there is anarchy or a possibility of anarchy.
The application to Hobbes's own times is obvious. The
king, for example, has a right to raise ship-money in
case of necessity. But who has a right to decide the
question of necessity? If the king, he could raise
taxes at pleasure. If the parliament, the king becomes
only their pensioner. At the bottom it was a question
of sovereignty, and Hobbes, holding the king to be
sovereign, holds that Hampden showed "an ignorant
impatience of taxation." "Mark the oppression! A
parliament man of £500 a year, land-taxed 20s."
Hampden was refusing to contribute to his own defence. "All men are by nature provided of notable
multiplying glasses, through which every little pay-
ment appeareth a great grievance." Parliament
remonstrated against arbitrary imprisonment, the Star
Chamber, and so forth; but it was their own fault
that the king had so to act. Their refusal to give
money "put him (the king) upon those extraordinary
ways, which they call illegal, of raising money at home."
The experience of the Civil War, he says in the
Leviathan, has so plainly shown the mischief of dividing
the rights of the sovereign that few men in England
fail to see that they should be inseparable and should
be so acknowledged "at the next return of peace."

Men did in fact come to acknowledge it, though not
for some generations, and then by virtually transferring

sovereignty from the king to the parliament. A
confused state of mind in the interval was implied in
the doctrine which long prevailed, of the importance of
a division between the legislative, executive, and
judicial powers, and in the doctrine that the British
constitution represented a judicious mixture of the
three elements, aristocracy, monarchy, and democracy,
whose conflicts were regulated by an admirable
system of checks and balances. Whatever truth may
have been expressed in such theories, they were
erroneous so far as inconsistent with Hobbes's doctrine.
A division of the governmental functions is of course
necessary, and different classes should be allowed to
exercise an influence upon the State. But the division
of functions must be consistent with the recognition of
a single authority which can regulate and correlate
their powers; and a contest between classes, which
do not in some way recognise a sovereign arbitrator,
leads to civil war or revolution. Who is the sovereign, for example, was the essential question which
in the revolt of the American colonies, and in the
secession of the Southern States had to be answered by
bullets. So long as that question is open, there is a
condition of unstable equilibrium or latent anarchy.
The State, as Hobbes puts it, should have only one
soul, or as we may say, the political organism should
have the unity corresponding to a vital principle.

The unity of the Leviathan seemed to imply arbitrary power. Since the king had the power of the
sword, said Hobbes, he must also have the power of
the purse. The logic might be good, but might be
applied the other way. The true Englishman was
determined not to pay the money till he knew how it

was to be spent; and complained of a loss of liberty if it was taken by force. Hobbes's reply to this is very forcible and clears his position. He agreed with Johnson that the cry for liberty was cant. What he asks, in his *De Cive*, is meant by liberty? If an exemption from the laws, it can exist in no government whatever. If it consist in having few laws, and only those such as are necessary to peace, there is no more liberty in a democracy than in a monarchy. What men really demand is not liberty but "dominion." People are deceived because in a democracy they have a greater share in public offices or in choosing the officers. It does not follow that they have more liberty in the sense of less law. Hobbes was putting his finger upon an ambiguity which has continued to flourish. Liberty may either mean that a man is not bound by law or that he is only bound by laws which he has made (or shared in making) himself. We are quite aware at the present day that a democracy may use the liberty, which in one sense it possesses, by making laws which are inconsistent with liberty in the other sense.

The problem, so much discussed in our times, as to the proper limits of government interference had not then excited attention. Hobbes seems to incline towards non-interference. Subjects grow rich, he says, by "the fruits of the earth and water, labour and thrift" (land, labour, and capital), and the laws should encourage industry and forbid extravagance. The "impotent" should be supported and the able-bodied set to work; taxes should be equal, and laid upon consumption, which (as he thinks) will encourage saving, and extravagance should be punished. So far his

principles are those which his contemporaries fully
accepted. But he adds, emphatically, that the laws
should not go too far. "As water enclosed on all
hands with banks, stands still and corrupts, so
subjects, if they might do nothing without the
command of the law, would grow dull and un-
wieldy." They must not, however, be left too much
to themselves. "Both extremes are faulty, for laws
were not invented to take away but to direct
men's actions, even as nature ordained the banks not
to stay, but to guide the course of the stream; it is
therefore against sound policy that there should be
more laws than necessarily serve for the good of the
magistrate and his subjects." Laws, moreover, should
be clear, simple, and directed not to revenge, but to
correction. "Leaders of a commotion should be
punished; not the poor seduced people. To be severe
to the people, is to punish that ignorance which may
in great part be imputed to the sovereign, whose fault
it was that they were no better instructed." This is,
perhaps, the only remark of Hobbes which would be
endorsed by Tolstoi. Hobbes was in favour of a
despotic rule; but he was anxious that it should be
thoroughly humane, and was fully sensible that the
English laws were in great need of reform.

Such questions, however, were then in the back-
ground. The real issue with his contemporaries was
different. Although his theory of sovereignty is
avowedly independent of the particular form of government, he has a leaning to monarchy. He confesses
that he has not proved this advantage demonstratively:
"the one thing in the whole book," he adds, in regard
to which he will make that modest admission. His

grounds are mainly that a king has a direct interest in promoting the welfare of his subjects, while popular leaders are prompted by vainglory and jealousy of each other, and popular assemblies are swayed by orators, for whom he always expresses contempt. "A democracy is no more than an aristocracy of orators, interrupted sometimes with the temporary monarchy of one orator": a Pym or a Gladstone. Hobbes's dislike to popular rule may be due in part to a certain intellectual difficulty. A sovereign must needs be a unit. But Hobbes is not comfortable with abstractions, or with so vague a body as the sovereign in a complex political system. He likes to have a king—a concrete, tangible individual in whom his principles may be incarnated. This prevents him from recognising one development of his theory which none the less was implied from the first. He perceives with perfect clearness and asserts in the most vigorous way that the division of sovereignty was the real weakness of the English system. His prejudices lead him to throw the whole blame upon the popular leaders. But a man of science should see that it is little to the purpose to blame individuals. Their discontent is a fact : a philosophical reformer should aim not at denouncing the symptoms, but at removing the causes of discord. It was clearly hopeless to persuade either side that it was in the wrong; but he might have tried to give an impartial diagnosis of the disease. He might then have admitted that the true solution might be, not to give the power of the purse to the king, but to give the power of the sword to the parliament. If he had contemplated that proposition, he might have foreseen (I do not mean that any human being could wholly

have foreseen) that his theory would apply to a
radically changed order.

In fact, Hobbes's Leviathan represents what is called
"the modern State." Supremacy of the law, absolute
authority of the governing power, and unity of the
administrative system may be most fully realised when
the "sovereign" is not an individual but an organic
body. Government represents or "bears the person
of the people," not in Hobbes's sense, that whatsoever
the sovereign wills becomes their will, but in the inverse
sense, that whatever they will becomes his will. Similar
consequences follow in either version. Hobbes, for
example, believes in the equality of man. It is one
of his laws of nature that "every man acknowledge
another for his equal by nature." Even if men were
not equal, they would only make the compact on conditions of equality. Inequality of subjects, he says
elsewhere, is made by the sovereign; and therefore
all must be equal before the sovereign, as kings and
subjects are equal before the King of Kings. Crimes
of great men are "not extenuated but aggravated by
the greatness of their persons." If they are favoured,
"impunity maketh insolence; insolence hatred; and
hatred an endeavour to pull down all oppressing and
contumelious greatness, though with the ruin of the
commonwealth." No subject can acquire any rights
which will impede the full exercise of the sovereign
power. The property of subjects in lands, for example,
"consisteth in right to exclude all other subjects from
the use of them, and not to exclude their sovereign,
be it an assembly or a monarch." If land is not to be
nationalised, the landowner's right is never absolute.
So in all "systems subject—that is, in all associations

of any kind—no power can be enjoyed except what the sovereign chooses to allow." They must be thoroughly subordinate to his will, though in practice they have an awkward tendency to independence. Among the diseases of a commonwealth, Hobbes reckons great towns able to furnish an army (London, of course, is in his mind) "as well as the great number of corporations which are, as it were, many lesser commonwealths in the bowels of the greater, like worms in the entrails of a natural man." The principle is evidently fatal to privileged estates or corporations. The king or sovereign may call in councillors; but they must remain councillors only. That, for example, is the case with the House of Commons. But the House of Lords has no better claim. "Good counsel comes not by inheritance." The claim of certain persons to have a place in the highest council by inheritance is derived "from the conquests of the ancient Germans." Their chiefs were able to extract privileges for their posterity. Such privileges, however, are inconsistent with sovereign power, and, if men contend for them as a right, they "must needs by degrees let them go," and be content with the honour due to their natural abilities.

This consequence of the supremacy of the sovereign illustrates one curious contrast between Hobbes and his opponents. The parliamentary party had to defend privilege against prerogative; and privilege has to be defended by precedent. The party, therefore, which would in modern phrase claim to be the "party of progress," justified itself by appealing to antiquity. When, indeed, you cut off a king's head you have to appeal to general principles. Constitutional precedents are not available. Milton had to claim indefeasible

rights for the people, and men like honest John Lil-
burne used language which anticipated Paine's *Rights
of Man*. But,in the earlier stages of the quarrel, Coke's
gigantic knowledge of old records, and superstitious
reverence for the common law, that is, for tradition
and custom, was a stronghold of the party. Hobbes
rejects the whole doctrine. An absolute political
theory could not fit into the constitutional tradition
or justify the heterogeneous products of historical
accidents. His treatise on the common law expresses
his aversion to Coke. He had already quoted him in
the *Leviathan* to show how men's judgments were
"perverted by trusting to precedent." "If the man
who first judged, judged unjustly, no injustice can be
a pattern of justice to succeeding judges." No custom,
again, can justify itself. If "use obtaineth the authority of a law, it is not the length of time that maketh
the authority, but the will of the sovereign signified
by his silence." The tacit consent of a ruler may make
a custom law. But "many unjust actions and unjust
sentences go uncontrolled for a longer time than any
man can remember." Only "reasonable" customs
should be law, and evil customs should be abolished.
The sovereign must decide what is reasonable and
what should be abolished.

According to Hobbes, then, all political machinery
is absolutely subordinate to the sovereign. His power
is the sole working force, and every resisting element
must be ejected or brought under control. The law
is the expression of his will, and,though he may enforce
rules which have grown up independently, they can
only exist on sufferance or by his tacit consent. In
that respect Hobbes was at one with the most thorough-

going revolutionists who ever proposed to rearrange
the political order upon an ideal plan, and to abolish
all traditional law which is not in conformity with the
dictates of reason.   As a matter of fact, Hobbes's
legal doctrine came to life again in the hands of
Bentham and his follower, Austin, the legal lights of
the "philosophical radicals."   Maine observes that
they had scarcely anything to add to Hobbes's analysis
of the meaning of law.   Hobbes puts his theory with
all possible clearness in the *De Cive* and the *Leviathan*.
"A law is a command of that person, whose precept
contains in it the reason of obedience."   The "civil
law" is the command of the sovereign.   We are bound
to obey it because it is his command, as soon as we
know it to be his.   It must therefore be promulgated
in order that we may know it, and have a "penalty
annexed to it" in order that we may obey it; for
"vain is that law which may be broken without
punishment."   When we are solemnly informed that
a law is a command of the sovereign, enforced by a
"sanction," the impulse of the unregenerate mind is
to reply, "that is what I always supposed."   Parliament and the policeman are phenomena too obvious to
be overlooked; the great manufactory which is always
turning out laws, and the rod which will smite us if
we do not obey, are always with us.   What else
should a law be than a rule made by one and enforced
by the other?   We are told in reply that great confusion has arisen by confounding such laws with "Laws
of Nature," laws which are supposed to exist in some
transcendental world, and yet to supply the necessary
basis for the laws of actual life, and which have to be
applied to life by the help of such shifty and ambigu-

ous hypotheses as the social contract. I do not doubt
that that is true, but it suggests one question. Austin
and his disciples were always exposing the absurdity
of the Law of Nature and the social contract, and yet
their own doctrine coincides with that of Hobbes, who
professes to make these theories an integral part of
his system.

The explanation is simple, and gives the essence
of Hobbes. According to Hobbes, in fact, the
Law of Nature has a singularly limited sphere of
action. It only exists, one may say, in order to repeal
itself. Before the social contract, he says, every man
has a right to everything, which is practically equivalent to nobody having a right to anything; for if the
same thing belongs to two men, neither has a right
against the other. But the contract is itself made by
every man resigning all his rights to the sovereign.
When he has thus made them over, he can no longer
make any claims under the Law of Nature. The
sovereign may command him to do anything (except,
indeed, to help to hang himself) and he is bound to
obey. The Law of Nature orders him to obey the
positive law, and does nothing else. This comes,
however, of being thoroughly logical, after making
one initial error. The Law of Nature is simply the
law of self-preservation, and whatever necessarily
follows from it. But in what sense of "law" can
we call self-preservation a law ? In one sense it is
what Hobbes calls a "theorem," not a law. It is
(assuming its truth) a statement of fact. All men
do aim at self-preservation. That is their one actual
and, indeed, their one possible principle. If so, it
cannot be a "law" at all in the ethical or strictly

legal sense. It expresses an essential condition of man's nature, and not a law imposed upon him from without. Men act for their own preservation as stones fall by gravitation. It is a way they have, and they cannot have any other. Taking for granted the truth of the "theorem," it will enable us to show how political institutions and "civil laws" have come into existence, but it does not show that they are right or wrong. It is as irrelevant to introduce that confusion as it would be to say that the angles of a triangle ought to be equal to two right angles. Hobbes's real theory comes out when we drop the imaginary contract altogether. We assume "self-preservation" as the universal instinct and, moreover, we must provisionally accept Hobbes's thoroughgoing egoism. Then so long as there is no common superior, the instinct produces competition and war, and implies the nasty, brutish "state of nature." How do men get out of it? Historically, he replies, governments may be made by conquest or developed out of the family, "which is a little monarchy." In both cases sovereignty is acquired by "force" and the subjects submit from fear. Governments, also, are made by "institution," that is, by the social contract; and in this case the motive is still fear, but fear of one another. Admitting, then, that even as an historical fact, sovereignty has been made by "institution" or contract, the essential motive is still the same. Each man sees that he will be better off, or preserve his life and means of living better, if he and his will obey a sovereign than if they remain masterless. The hypothesis that States were deliberately contrived and made by a bargain between the separate atoms is, of course, absurd historically, but is also irrelevant to Hobbes. The essential point is simply that settled order is so much more favourable to self-preservation than anarchy that every one has a sufficient interest in maintaining it. Peace, as he tells us, means all the arts and sciences that distinguish Europeans from Choctaws. The original contractors can scarcely be supposed to have foreseen that. But at least it gives a very good reason for obedience.

This comes out curiously in Hobbes's "exceptions" to the obligation of the contract. Men are not bound to kill themselves, because the tacit "consideration" for accepting the contract was the preservation of life and the means of life. He was logically bound to go further. If upon that ground they may repudiate the contract, they may break it whenever the end is frustrated, that is, whenever by keeping it they will be in a worse position. Moreover, since nobody ever acts except for his own good, they certainly will break it whether it is binding or not. In other words, the supposed contract is merely another version of the first principle of egoism : a man will always do what seems to be for his own interest. By calling it a contract he gets the appearance of extending the obligation to a wider sphere—to cases, that is, in which a man's interest is opposed to his contract. But it is only an appearance. It is indeed true that, when a sovereign has once been set up, fraud and force cease to pay, as a general rule, and honesty becomes the best policy. But that is more simply expressed without reference to a contract. It merely means that the most selfish of mankind finds that it is worth while to have a policeman round the corner. Indeed, the more selfish he is the greater may be the convenience. By abandoning my supposed right to all things, I get an effectual right to most things ; and that may be called a bargain, but it is a bargain which I shall only keep, and indeed can only keep, according to Hobbes, so long as the balance of profit is on my side. That is, it is not a bargain at all.

The facts, however, remain, and Hobbes manages to state a clear and coherent scheme. His position may be compared to that of the old economists. They used to maintain that in taking for granted the selfishness of mankind they were making a legitimate abstraction. Men, it is true, are not simply selfish, they have other motives than a love of money ; but the love of money is so prominent an instinct in economic masses that we may consider it as the sole force at work, and so we may get a theory which will be approximately true, though requiring correction when applied to concrete cases. Hobbes virtually considers the political system in so far as it is based upon selfish motives and is worked by individual interests. No doubt such motives are tolerably prevalent. The obvious and most assignable motive for obeying the law is fear of the hangman ; and all manner of selfish interests are furthered by maintaining a settled system of government. He thus obtains a clear conception of one important aspect of the political order. It means organised force. The State is held together by armies which protect us from invasion, and by the administrative system which preserves order at home. These are undeniable facts which it is as well to recognise clearly, and which are most vigorously set forth in Hobbes's *Leviathan*.

Certain limits to the value of his theory are equally plain. In the *Leviathan* Hobbes says that the "public ministers" are parts organical of the commonwealth, and compares the judges to the "organs of voice," the executive to the hands, ambassadors to eyes, and so forth. The analogy between the political, and the individual organism is implied in the whole theory. But the Leviathan is an "artificial" body, and "artificial" means mechanical construction. The individual is the ultimate unit, and though he resigns his rights to the sovereign, it is always for his own personal advantage. The comparison to a body suggests the modern phrase "the social organism," but the "artificial" indicates that Hobbes does not really interpret the Leviathan as an organism. It is a big machine or set of atoms held together by external bonds. Hobbes's egoism forces him to the doctrine that the particles gravitate together simply from fear—fear of the magistrate or fear of your neighbour. Sympathy is ignored, and such sentiments as patriotism or public spirit or philanthropy are superficial modifications of selfishness, implying a readiness to adopt certain precautions for securing our own lives and properties. This involves a one-sided view of the conditions of social and political welfare. It may be fully admitted that organised force is essential to a civilised society, that it cannot exist or develop without its military and judicial bodies, its soldiers and its judges, its hangmen, gaolers, and policemen, its whole protective apparatus. An animal cannot live without its teeth and claws. What is overlooked is the truth that other parts of the system are equally essential, and that there is a reciprocal dependence indicated by the word "organic." Society is held

together not simply by the legal sanctions, but by all
the countless instincts and sympathies which bind men
together, and by the spontaneous associations which
have their sources outside of the political order.   It
may be granted to Hobbes that peace is an essential
condition of progress, and that the sovereign must be
created to keep the peace.   It is equally true that the
sovereign derives his power from other sources than
mutual "fear" or dread of the "legal sanctions."
Society could not get on without the policeman; but
the policeman could not keep order by the simple force
of his truncheon.   Force must be "organised," but it
cannot be organised out of simple egoism and fear.
So when Hobbes defines law as the command of the
sovereign, he is stating what in a fully developed State
is an undeniable fact.   The law is the system of rules
promulgated and enforced by the sovereign power in
spite of any conflicting customs.   Historically speaking,
laws are not the less the product of customs which
have grown up spontaneously; they are the causes, not
the effects of the sovereign's authority; and in the
last resort the sovereign power must still rest upon
custom; that is, upon all the complex motives from
which arises loyalty to the State, and upon which its
vitality depends.

Hobbes's position was indeed inevitable. The conception of sociology as a science, in which the political
order is regarded as only part of the whole social
system, had not yet arisen.   That could not happen
until historical methods of inquiry had begun to show
their power, and the necessity of treating political
questions in connection with the intellectual or the
industrial evolution began to be perceived.   The

"social contract" theory helped Hobbes to pass over in
summary fashion the great historical problems as to the
way in which the State has actually been developed;
and therefore the State itself could be regarded as held
together by the purely political and legal forces.
When he had deduced the sovereign power from the
principle of self-preservation, he seemed to himself to
have explained everything. He had got to the one
force which held the units together, as gravitation holds
together the solar system. The relation between subject and sovereign is the one bond from which all
others may be deduced. The thoroughgoing acceptance of this assumption leads to some of the singular
results by which he startled his contemporaries,
though he announces them with superlative calmness
as demonstrated truths.

There are, as he has to admit, two sets of laws
which may occasionally conflict with the laws of
the State. In the first place, there is the moral law.
Hobbes was perfectly well aware that a king might be
a fool or a brute. It seemed to follow that laws might
be contrary to the dictates of morality. His opponents
could point out to him that some of the Roman
emperors had been far from model characters. Besides
their other weaknesses, they had occasionally thought
it right to give Christians to lions. Again, the Christian
Church claimed obedience, and Hobbes was an orthodox Christian. What is the subject to do if his
sovereign orders him to break the moral law or to deny
the truth of religion?

4. *The Moral Law.*

Hobbes does not shrink from the logical result

of his principles. The moral law, he holds, is the Law of Nature. The Law of Nature, as we have seen, means essentially the law of self - preservation, and from that is deduced the "virtue" of justice, from which all other laws of nature are corollaries. Justice means keeping covenants, which becomes operative when a "coercive power" is constituted; that is, at the institution of the social contract. This contract therefore is at the base of all moral as well as of all political relations. It is presupposed in all particular contracts. Justice, the cardinal or rather the sole virtue, means keeping covenants, but also keeping the primitive contract to which all others owe their binding force. It implies, therefore, unconditional obedience to the sovereign who is the social contract incarnate. The sovereign cannot be unjust to a subject; for every subject is himself author of all that the sovereign does. Laws are the "rules of just and unjust; nothing being reputed unjust that is not contrary to some law." "The Law of Nature and the civil law contain each other and are of equal extent." "Justice, gratitude, and other moral virtues" are merely "qualities that dispose men to peace and obedience" until the commonwealth is instituted. Then they become laws, "for it is the sovereign power that obliges men to obey them." Thus the Law of Nature is part of the civil law, and "reciprocally the civil law is part of the dictates of nature."

Nobody, I believe, ever followed Hobbes in this audacious identification of law and morality. I must try to make some apology for a most estimable old gentleman misled by an excessive passion for logic. In the first place, it may be held that, whatever be the

ultimate meaning of morality, the actual morality of a
race is evolved in constant correlation with its social
organisation. Hobbes, who substituted the social contract for this process, and regarded sovereignty as
the sole bond of union, could only approximate to this
doctrine by making moral obligations a product of the
sovereign will. It would be outrageous, no doubt, to
suppose that a sovereign could make the moral law at
his pleasure, so that lying might become a virtue or
gratitude a vice if the lawgiver chose to alter the law.
That is not Hobbes's meaning. Honesty, gratitude, and
the like are, we see, useful qualities and parts of the
Law of Nature as tending to self-preservation. The
sovereign of course cannot alter that fact. What he
can do is to make them obligatory by establishing the
state of security which makes their exercise possible or
prudent for the individual. In the "state of nature"
the conduct would be self-destructive, which, when the
commonwealth is formed, becomes self-preservative.
But, we may ask, Will the power thus constituted aim
at the end for which it was instituted ? May not the
sovereign do wrong ? May he not be a brutal tyrant,
or lay down laws which are immoral, because inconsistent with the welfare of the people ? Is it in that
case our duty to obey them ? Must we submit to
oppression or enslave our neighbours because the
sovereign, whether king or parliament, commands it ?
Hobbes admits the possibility. "They that have the
sovereign power may commit iniquity, but not injustice
or injury in the proper signification." That is, the
sovereign's immorality gives no right to the subject to
disobey or even to protest. The reason is that the
only alternative is anarchy. Bad laws are better than

no laws. "Good," as we have seen, means what a man desires and evil what he eschews. "One counts that good which another counts evil; and the same man what now he esteemed for good, he immediately after looks on as evil; and the same thing which he calls good in himself he terms evil in another." There is no such thing as absolute good. Hence it is impossible to make a common rule from the tastes of "particular" men. We have to consider what is reasonable; but "there are no other reasons in being but those of particular men and that of the city; it follows that the city is to determine what with reason is culpable." We are bound to obey the laws before we know what the laws are; for the State must precede the law. Therefore "no civil law whatever can be against the Law of Nature." The Law of Nature may forbid theft and adultery; but till we have civil laws we do not know what theft and adultery are. When the Spartans permitted their youth to take other men's goods, the taking was not theft. In other words, all law becomes positive law, for the Law of Nature only orders us to obey the law of the sovereign. It has been said that "whatsoever a man does against his conscience is sin." That is true in the "state of nature," where a man has no rule but his own reason. "It is not so with him that lives in a commonwealth, because the law is the public conscience by which he hath already undertaken to be guided." Otherwise nobody would obey further than it seemed good in his own eyes.

The subject, then, hands over the whole responsibility to the sovereign. Then "it is in the laws of a commonwealth as it is in the laws of gaming; whatso-

ever the gamesters all agree on is injustice to none of
them." Are then the laws as arbitrary as the laws of
a game ? To that Hobbes has his answer : "The safety
of the people is the supreme law." The sovereign is
"obliged by the Law of Nature" to procure this end,
"and to render an account thereof to God and to none
but Him." Remembering the peculiarity of Hobbes's
theology, it may seem that this responsibility is perhaps illusory. It is more to his purpose that, as he
puts it, "the good of the sovereign and people cannot
be separated." "It is a weak sovereign that has weak
subjects, and a weak people whose sovereign wanteth
power to rule them at his will." It is clearly to the
interest of the sovereign, as it is also his duty, to maintain order. But to maintain order is, according to
Hobbes, to enforce morality. The sovereign has to
instruct his people in the "fundamental rights" of his
office. To do so is "not only his duty, but his benefit
also, and security against the danger that may arise to
himself in his natural person from rebellion." He proceeds in his quaint fashion to point out that this duty
of instructing the people is the duty of impressing
upon them the Ten Commandments. Since kings are
mortal gods, the commandments of the first table are
applicable to them as well as to the Supreme Being.
Clearly a man who proves that kings not only should
but naturally will adopt the Ten Commandments is
preaching a sound morality.

It is necessary, however, to remember Hobbes's
general ethical conception. Every man acts simply
for his own good. Every man, again, interprets
"good" as that which pleases him. Order can only be
established when every man sees that he will get more

good for himself by submitting to a common authority.
When that is securely established, the individual will
be repaid for sacrificing that right to everything
which he could not enforce. But, when that is done,
the moral law is made supreme. For morality, according to Hobbes, is summed up in justice; that is, in
observing the general contract according to which the
distribution of good things is regulated and men are
obliged to keep their particular contracts. Equality
before the law and equality of taxation are also implied,
for inequality leads to discontent. But in other
respects every man may, and of course will, be guided
by his own conceptions of "good." As I have said
before, Hobbes is not in favour of extending the
sphere of legislation. Laws are "like hedges," set
"not to stop travellers but to keep them in their way.
And therefore a law which is not needful, having not
the true end of law, is not good." "Unnecessary
laws are not good laws, but traps for money; which,
where the right of sovereign power is acknowledged,
are superfluous; and, where it is not acknowledged,
insufficient to defend the people."

This, it seems, is the essential meaning of Hobbes's
identification of law and morality. They are, according to him, different aspects of the virtue which he
calls justice. That means that a man acts morally, so
far as he pursues his own ends without harming his
neighbour; and legally, so far as he obeys the sovereign who enforces the security without which it is
not a man's interest to act morally. No doubt this is
a totally inadequate view of morality. It is the legal
or purely external conception which supposes that the
moral, like the positive, law is satisfied by obeying

certain "sanctions" which make bad conduct unprofit-
able. But it does not imply that the moral law is
"arbitrary" or made at will by the sovereign. It is
the law of "self-preservation" regarded from a purely
egoistic point of view.

5. *The Spiritual Power.*

Hobbes's theory may lead to some pretty problems
in casuistry. How far should a man's duty to the
State override the dictates of his conscience? May a
soldier refuse to serve in a war that he thinks unjust?
Or a Quaker refuse to fight at all? May a man refuse
to pay taxes if he disapproves of the purpose for
which they are raised? To admit such liberty unreservedly is to approve of anarchy, and upon that
ground some people become anarchists. The problem,
however, does not often present itself in practice.
Most laws are sufficiently in conformity with the
average morality of the people to excite no protest.
But another question was far more pressing, and to
Hobbes seemed to be the really critical question of
the day. What is to be done when the subject's
religious convictions clash with his obligations to the
State? To that problem Hobbes gave an answer in
his first treatise, which was expanded in the *De Cive*,
and given at great length and with many singular
developments in the *Leviathan.*

His essential position is simple enough: the sovereign has to keep the peace. Now men's "actions
proceed from their opinions," and therefore opinions
must be governed in order to govern action, and
governed in the interests of peace. He agrees

that in speculation "nothing ought to be regarded but the truth." True opinion, however, cannot be "repugnant to peace." "Yet the most sudden and rough bursting in of a new truth, that can be, does never break the peace but only sometimes awake the the war"; that is, where error is already prevalent and people are ready to fight for it. It follows that the suppression of an opinion "repugnant to peace" must also be the suppression of error. He limits the suppression, however, to the public teaching, through books or otherwise, of objectionable opinions, for he also holds that a man's private beliefs cannot be determined by force. The sovereign is therefore bound to forbid the open propagation of opinions by which his authority is subverted. The diseases which bring about the "dissolution of commonwealths" are seditious opinions. Besides the opinion that every private man is to judge of good and evil, there is the opinion that a man may claim supernatural inspiration: a pernicious doctrine which in this part of the world has been turned to account by "unlearned divines," sufficiently prevalent in the fanatical sects of the commonwealth.

But a still more vital power is represented by the claims of the papacy. This, in fact, means the cardinal error of a divided sovereignty. It is a setting up of "*supremacy* against *sovereignty*; *canons* against *laws*, and a ghostly authority against the civil." "Now seeing it is manifest that the civil power and the power of the commonwealth is the same thing, and that supremacy and the power of making canons . . . implieth a commonwealth, it followeth that where one is sovereign, another supreme—where one can make

laws and another make canons—there must needs be
two commonwealths of one and the same subjects,
which is a kingdom divided against itself and cannot
stand." The "ghostly power challengeth the right
to declare what is sin," and therefore the right to
declare what is law, for sin is "nothing but the trans-
gression of the law." As the civil power also declares
what is law, it follows either that every subject must
obey two masters, or that one of the two powers
must be subordinate to the other. The civil authority
has the advantage of being "more visible"; but the
spiritual, though it deals in unintelligible doctrines,
yet, "because the fear of darkness and ghosts is
greater than other fears, cannot want a party sufficient
to trouble and sometimes to destroy a commonwealth."
The spiritual power, indeed, has an advantage, "for
every man" (as he says in the *De Cive*), "if he be
in his wits, will in all things yield that man an
absolute obedience, by virtue of whose sentence he
believes himself to be either saved or damned."
Church or State, that is, must be supreme, or there
will be a fatal disease which he quaintly compares to
the epilepsy, a "wind in the head," which makes men
fall into fire or water. When the spiritual power
moves the subject "by the terror of punishment and
hope of reward" of this supernatural kind, "and by
strange and hard words suffocates their understanding,
it must needs thereby distract the people, and either
overwhelm the commonwealth by oppression or cast it
into the fire of a civil war." Which then is to be
supreme? A Church, like a State, must be an organised
body and have a sovereign before it can be said to
"will" or "command." He defines it therefore as a

"company of men professing Christian religion united
in the person of one sovereign, at whose command
they ought to assemble, and without whose authority
they ought not to assemble." Now, in all commonwealths, an assembly in order to be lawful must have
the warrant of the civil sovereign. There is no power
on earth to which all commonwealths are subject, and
the Christians in each State are subject to its sovereign
and cannot be subject to any other power. Therefore
a Church is the same thing with the civil commonwealth, which is "called a civil state, for that the
subjects of it are men, and a church, for that the
subjects thereof are Christians." "Temporal" and
"spiritual" are "two words brought into the world
to make men see double and mistake their lawful
sovereign." Unless there is one governor there will
be civil war between Church and State—"between
the sword of justice and the shield of faith—and, which
is more, in every Christian man's own breast between
the Christian and the man."

The Church, in short, as a law-making or governing
body must be fused with the State. Otherwise we
have the fatal splitting of sovereignty. An antagonist
might have replied that the unity might be equally
secured by subordinating the State to the Church.
An absolute theocracy, such as corresponded to the
extremest claims of the papacy, would have satisfied
the condition as fully as the secular sovereignty. To
this Hobbes replies upon the historical ground. He
denies that the Church of Rome, or indeed, that the
spiritual power from the beginning of the world can
make out any title to the sovereign power. Half of
the *Leviathan*, namely the third part ("Of a Christian

Commonwealth ") and the fourth (" Of the Kingdom
of Darkness ") is devoted to this argument.

It is a most singular performance. Hobbes has to
argue from the Bible, and quotes texts as confidently
as any contemporary divine. He protests, indeed,
with an air of perfect candour, that he has only taken
the plainest sense and that which is "agreeable to the
harmony and scope of the whole Bible." But his
exegesis brings out results which nobody before or
since has ever deduced from the same authority. We
may wonder whether he is sincere or laughing in
his sleeve; whether, perhaps, he means simply an
argument *ad hominem*; or a tacit suggestion that any
conclusions you please can be extorted from the
documents whose authority he is bound to admit.
Our confidence is not increased by his apology for his
paradoxes. He admits that one doctrine, which he
proves, will appear to most men a novelty. "I do but
propound it," he says, "maintaining nothing in this or
any other paradox of religion, but attending the end
of that dispute of the sword concerning the authority,
not yet amongst my countrymen decided, by which all
sorts of doctrine are to be approved or rejected." Anyhow the results are too grotesque to be given at
length, or to be quite passed over.

His contention is essentially that there never was
a divinely instituted spiritual authority independent
of the civil authority. The civil and ecclesiastical
powers, for example, were united in Abraham, afterwards in Moses, and then in the high priests. "Whoever had the sovereignty of the commonwealth among
the Jews, the same had also the supreme authority in
the matter of God's external worship," though the

Jews got into many calamities from not properly understanding the rights of their rulers. The old dispensation, it might be supposed, was superseded by the Christian Church, and its rulers would represent Christ on earth. But "the Kingdom of Christ" was not of this world. That, according to Hobbes, means that it will not be established until a new world begins upon "the general resurrection." Then Christ will become a King in the literal sense. The good will come to life in their old bodies (for there is no such thing as a separate soul) and live eternally. They will not marry or be given in marriage, for otherwise the earth would obviously not be big enough to hold the resulting population. There will be no death vacancies. The wicked will also come to life in order to receive condign punishment. They will suffer "the second death," which cannot, as he thinks, mean eternal life in torture, but simple extinction. As they will die, they may propagate; and therefore hell may be eternal in the sense that there will always be a supply of the wicked to be punished, though every individual will come to an end. This amazing theory is meant to show that since Christ's kingdom is not to become a reality until the resurrection, the Church is, for the time being, not a kingdom at all but a mere voluntary association. The apostles and their successors could only persuade, not command, and had no coercive powers. Excommunication could only mean amicable separation, not the infliction of a penalty. The Church did not acquire legal authority until it was invested with power by the emperor.

These queer speculations are connected with a more

P

interesting set of arguments. Hobbes wishes to meet
the claims of the Church to supernatural authority.
He cannot deny—explicitly at any rate—that Moses
and the prophets were divinely inspired. What he can
do is to argue that their inspiration does not transmit
supernatural authority to their descendants. Moses
himself knew that he was speaking to Jehovah. But
in what way Jehovah spoke to him is "not intelligible."
The Jews could only know that Moses told them that
he was so speaking, and that makes a vital difference.
When a prophet says that God has spoken to him in
a dream, that is only to say he "dreamed that God
spoke to him, which is not of force to win belief from
any man that knows that dreams are for the most
part natural." To say that a man speaks by "supernatural inspiration is to say he finds an ardent desire
to speak in some strong opinion of himself, for which
he can allege no natural and sufficient reason. So that,
though God Almighty can speak to a man by dreams,
visions, voice, and inspiration, yet he obliges no man
to believe he hath so done to him that pretends it,
who, being a man, may err, and which is more, may
lie." As miracles have ceased, we can now only appeal
to the Holy Scriptures. What, then, is the authority
of the Scriptures? Hobbes goes through many of the
passages, which have been mentioned by later critics,
to show that the books ascribed to Moses and others
were written after the time of the supposed authors.
The Psalter must have been put into its present form
after the captivity, as some of the psalms refer to it.
The authority of the Old Testament in general can
only be traced to the time of Esdras, who discovered
the books when they were lost; and the canon of

the New Testament cannot be proved to have been
authoritative before the Council of Laodicea in the
year 364 A.D. Hobbes, indeed, believes that the New
Testament books are genuine, for a characteristic
reason : The doctors of the Church had claimed
supreme power by the time of the Council and
thought pious frauds commendable. If they had
altered the books "they would surely have made
them more favourable to their power over Christian
princes . . . than they are." Why, then, do we believe
the Scriptures to be the Word of God? Everybody,
he says, admits the fact of inspiration, but no one
can know it except "those to whom God himself hath revealed it supernaturally." Men believe,
though they do not know, for reasons so various
that no general account of them can be given. But
"the question truly stated is, by what authority they
(the Scriptures) are made law." The answer is
obvious. They must be imposed by a sovereign
authority; and, if so, either by sovereigns each
absolute in his own territory, or by the "Vicar of
Christ" as sovereign of the universal Church, who
must then have the power of judging, deposing, or
putting to death the subordinate sovereigns. Meanwhile, every man is "bound to make use of his
natural reason" to test the claims of a prophet. It
is clear that a great many prophets are not to be
trusted. When Ahab consulted four hundred prophets, all but one were impostors, "and a little
before the time of the captivity the prophets were
generally liars (see Jeremiah xiv. 14)." We must
judge them then by their conformity to the established authority. When Christians do not take their

own sovereign for God's prophet, they must take
their own dreams or obey "some strange prince," or
be bewitched into rebellion and the "chaos of violence
and civil war" by some fellow-subject.

Hobbes proceeds to treat of miracles. We take
an event to be miraculous when we do not perceive
its cause. The first rainbow "was a miracle because
the first," and consequently strange. A rainbow is
not a miracle now, because it is no longer strange,
even to those who do not know the cause. That
may be a miracle to one man which is not so to
another. Before astronomy became a science, a man
who predicted an eclipse would pass for a prophet.
Juggling, ventriloquism, and thaumaturgy are common,
and "there is nothing how impossible soever to be
done that is impossible to be believed." When we
hear of a miracle, we must therefore consult the
lawful head of the Church how far we are to give
credit to the story. "A private man has always
the liberty, because thought is free, to believe or
not believe in his heart those acts that have been
given out for miracles," and he should consider who
is likely to profit by them. "But when it comes
to the confession of that faith, the private reason
must submit to the public, that is to say, to God's
lieutenant."

Hobbes was thus suggesting doubts as to the
evidences of the established creeds, doubts which
were to bear fruit in a later generation. Spinoza,
in the *Tractatus Theologico-Politicus*, treated the questions on wider grounds and "went a bar" beyond
what Hobbes has dared to say. No active controversy, however, arose till a later period. Hobbes's

argument, we may notice, has a resemblance to
that which Hume made famous. Both of them
argue, not that miracles are impossible, but that the
proof of a miracle is always insufficient. Hobbes
has to assert that the events recorded in the Scriptures really happened, but endeavours to show that
there is no proof that they happened. We must
believe on authority, and, moreover, on the authority
of the Church. Only, by authority we do not mean
the intellectual authority of competent inquirers, but
the legal authority of the sovereign. Rather, we may
believe what we like, but we may only profess the
belief which the law allows us to profess.

We have still to see why he rejects the alternative
of the supremacy of the Church. The existing commonwealths are independent of each other, and therefore
not subject in fact to any central authority; but it
may still be urged that they ought to be subject to
this. To this he replies partly by the familiar Protestant arguments from texts, and maintains that
Bellarmine's interpretations of "feed my sheep," and
so forth, are erroneous. But the main answer is given
in the last book upon "The Kingdom of Darkness."
There he takes up the position which was already
assumed in his account of the natural history of religion. The gods of the heathen are, as we have
seen, mere "phantasms"—dreams mistaken for reality
and so forth. The Church of Rome adopted the same
methods. By misinterpreting Scripture the priests
made people believe in devils and exorcism, in
purgatory and the efficiency of sacraments, and other
doctrines calculated to increase their power and give
them authority over the secular rulers. They adopted

many ceremonies and superstitions from the Gentiles,
and they introduced the vain and erroneous philosophy
of Aristotle to perplex men's minds. The argument
ends by a quaint comparison between the papacy and
the "kingdom of fairies." The whole "hierarchy" has
been built up like the "old wives' fables in England
concerning ghosts and spirits and the feats they play in
the night." It is needless to go into the details; but
I may quote the striking phrase which sums up his
theory. "If a man consider the original of this great
ecclesiastical dominion, he will easily perceive that the
papacy is no other than the ghost of the deceased
Roman empire sitting crowned upon the grave thereof." "The Roman Church," says a great living
authority, "in this way privily pushed itself into the
place of the Roman world-empire of which it is the
historical continuation." [1] A comparison of the phrases
may illustrate Hobbes's vigorous grasp of thought as
well as command of words.

His ascription of sovereignty in religious matters to
the civil authority was startling enough, and led him
into some difficulties. What, for example, are we to
say of the Christian martyrs? They were clearly
rebels, and yet have been generally praised for their
conduct. Hobbes has to "distinguish." To be a true
martyr, a man must have "received a calling to
preach." He must, moreover, have seen the facts to
which he testifies. If he testifies to the resurrection,
he must have conversed with Christ before his death
and seen him after he was risen. Otherwise he can
only be a "martyr" (that is, a witness) to other men's

---

[1] Harnack's *What is Christianity?* p. 252.

testimony. Moreover, there is only one article for which a man ought to die, namely, that "Jesus is the Christ." We are not to die for every private tenet of our own or for tenets which suit the clergy. Naaman set a very convenient precedent, and if, like him, we obey our sovereign in using words which do not express our thoughts, the action is not ours but our sovereign's. To resist an infidel sovereign is to "sin against the laws of God (for such are the laws of nature) and the council of the apostles" (*i.e.* to obey princes). If we do not take Naaman's view, we must expect our reward in heaven. "But," he asks, "what infidel king is so unreasonable as, knowing he has a subject that waiteth for the second coming of Christ after the present world shall be burnt, and intendeth then to obey him (which is the intent of believing that Jesus is the Christ), and in the meantime thinketh himself bound to obey the laws of that infidel king (which all Christians are obliged in conscience to do), to put to death or persecute such a subject?" Certainly if all that is meant by belief in Christ is an intention of obeying him as a king after the general resurrection, the infidel king would be very unreasonable. They sometimes are.

Hobbes sums up his belief in one phrase. "Religion," he says, in dedicating his *Seven Problems* to Charles II., "is not philosophy but law." We have already seen what is the view which he takes in his natural history of religion. Religion is the "fear of power invisible." That is the essential meaning of the instinct, and legislators have taken advantage of it to strengthen their own authority and to keep the peace. Whether the objects of worship be real or "phantasms,"

religion is useful just so far as it promotes that end.
We know nothing of God except His power; and it is
upon His power that His authority is founded. All
the other attributes ascribed to him "are not to declare
what He is," but how much we honour Him. "The end
of worship among men is power." The worship of
God is directed by "those rules of honour that reason
dictateth to be done by the weak to the more potent
men in hope of benefit," or for fear of damage, or
thankfulness for good received. Prayer and thanks
are simply an acknowledgment of God's power.
Rational worship "argues a fear of Him, and fear
is a confession of His power." I will not ask
whether Hobbes's theological conceptions would
really justify even this account of religion. It
comes apparently to this : that religion is a system of
beliefs and observances imposed by the sovereign in
order to give force to the "Law of Nature," that is, the
law of self-preservation and the obligation of the social
contract. Modern thinkers have given a good many
definitions of religion; but this I fancy is not among
them.

Hobbes's purpose is clear enough. The Church, as he
holds, is an organised body which has taken advantage
of phantasms and dreams to claim supernatural powers
and to forge a system of spiritual weapons capable of
encountering the secular weapons of the sovereign.
Then it has elaborated the sham philosophy of the
schoolmen, the *empusa* which strangles thought by
words and enables it to bewilder men by mysterious
dogmas which are really nonsense. In attacking the
Church, therefore, he is defending the cause of enlight-
enment against a systematic obscurantism. He traces

the growth of the spiritual power through three stages:
first, the claim of priests to make belief obligatory
instead of free; secondly, the concentration of this
power in the hands of bishops; and thirdly, absorption
of the episcopal in the papal power. Queen Elizabeth
got rid of the pope; the Presbyterians of the bishops;
and the Presbyterians have now lost their power, so
that "we are reduced to the independency of the
primitive Christians," every man believing what he
pleases. This, he says, "is perhaps the best," first,
because there ought to be no power "over the consciences of men, but of the Word itself, working faith
in every man"; and secondly, because it is unreasonable
to ask a man to accept the reasons of others, "which
is little better than to venture his salvation at cross
and pile." Priests ought to know that power is preserved by the same virtues by which it is acquired—
"that is to say, by wisdom, humility, clearness of
doctrine, and sincerity of conversation; and not by
suppression of the natural sciences and of the morality
of natural reason; nor by obscure language; nor by
arrogating to themselves more knowledge than they
make appear; nor by pious frauds"; nor by other faults
which tend to scandal. Hobbes would thus seem to be
in favour of complete religious toleration and absolute
indifference of the State in religious matters. How is
this reconcilable with the theory that "religion is
law"?

The explanation is not far to seek. The endless
religious controversies had been made an argument on
one side for the necessity of a central spiritual
authority, and on the other for a limitation of the
essentials of religious belief to the points upon which

all men were agreed. Hobbes having, in words at
least, to accept the Christian doctrines, declares that
the only article of faith "which the Scripture maketh
simply necessary to salvation is this, that Jesus is the
Christ": an article which, as we have seen, he manipu-
lates strangely enough.   Other dogmas need not
trouble us.   "For it is with the mysteries of our
religion as with wholesome pills for the sick; which
swallowed whole have the virtue to cure; but chewed
are for the most part cast up again without effect."
Now when the State orders us to swallow, it will
allow us to take our pills whole.   The State, as he
says, can only take notice of our words.   It is one of
the vital errors of the false teachers to "extend the
power of the law to the very thoughts and consciences
of men."   That, he intimates, means the Inquisition,
which he detests as heartily as any man.   The only
interest of the State is in peace.   The secular
sovereign will not want to rouse theological quarrels
or to burn his subjects to enforce dogmas. Persecution
is the natural consequence when a great corporation
has been built up upon the ground of a dogmatic
system, and when all its interests depend upon en-
forcing orthodoxy.   The destruction of such a power
is Hobbes's real aim.   If we subordinate the Church to
the State, the secular sovereign will be no longer the
tool of the priest, and, even if he prescribes the verbal
acceptance of certain dogmas, he will take care that
they do no harm.   His aim will be to suppress controversy, not to hinder speculation.

The doctrine of toleration was developing, though
slowly enough, and Hobbes saw one difficulty clearly.
If by "religion" we mean simply the creed of the

individual, the case for toleration is obvious and over-powering. It must be wrong, that is, to punish a man for accepting what he believes to be true. But a practical difficulty remains when "religion" is regarded as the creed of an organised body, which has therefore a system of laws. What is to be done when such laws come into conflict with the laws of the State? The difficulty need not occur if as a matter of fact the Church and State do not represent conflicting theories, or if there be an agreement as to a demarcation of their spheres of action. But as religious motives affect men's conduct as a whole, the Church can hardly be indifferent to every part of the action of the State. When differences occur, as for example when the State undertakes the charge of education, there is even in our own day a great difficulty in applying the principle of toleration, however much it may be accepted in general terms. In Hobbes's time, such difficulties were of course much greater. The Puritan proposed to alter the constitution of the Church, but not to diminish its authority or to divorce it from the State. As sects multiplied, the principle of toleration became more widely accepted; for it is plain that when you are in a minority of one your only logical plea for liberty must imply universal toleration. Meanwhile Hobbes, disgusted by the struggles of rival sects and the claims of the Catholic church to interfere with political matters in the interest of the hated dogmatic system, took a short cut to a solution. Instead of trying to effect a reconciliation, he would simply put one power under the feet of the other, and the dominant power should be that which is least given to bigotry.

In some respects Hobbes's solution was that which

actually succeeded. The claim of the pope to depose
kings was of little practical importance; and Hobbes,
like his countrymen, seems to have been unduly
nervous. Giant Pope, though far from being so
decrepit as Bunyan thought, was ceasing to have much
authority over the political world. The Church of
England was following the course which Hobbes
desired. He complains that the bishops made certain
claims to independent authority, but remarks that at
any rate they had practically submitted to the king.
That tendency developed, and Hobbes would have
been thoroughly content with the eighteenth century,
when the Church ceased to make any claim to corporate
power, and the clergy became useful dependants on the
possessors of patronage.

NOTE

DURING the last months of his life Sir Leslie Stephen was writing this book. When he could no longer work he asked me to see it through the press. Its readers should, I think, be told that he had some thoughts of adding to it a few sentences about the influence exercised by Hobbes on later philosophers, the French Encyclopædists and the English Utilitarians, and that he gave me some notes, by the aid of which this addition might have been made. However, before his death I had sent him word that the book was so complete that no second hand ought to touch it. I have only made those small changes that must always be made whenever a book is printed. He expressly charged me to acknowledge his debt of gratitude to three of his precursors: his friend Croom Robertson, Dr. F. Tönnies, and M. Georges Lyon.

F. W. Maitland.

INDEX

pupil, 16; first acquaintance with Euclid, 17, 70, 71, 77, 80; inquiries into the nature of motion, 18, 21, 77, 78, 80; devotes himself seriously to philosophy, 19; renews his connection with the Cavendish family, 19, 20; further travels, 20; recognised by contemporary philosophers, 20; new acquaintances at home and abroad, 20, 21, 25; circulates summary of his philosophical ideas, 27; goes to France for greater safety, 27; controversy with Descartes, 33; publishes *De Cive*, 34; begins to write *The Leviathan*, 34; tutor to the exiled Prince of Wales, 38; severe illness, 40; publication of *The Leviathan*, 40; returns to England, 41, 45; accused of inconsistency and disloyalty, 41, 42, 43, 54; suspected of atheism, 44, 45, 59, 60, 67-9, 144, 150, 154; makes acquaintance of various distinguished men, 46-49; controversy with Bishop Bramhall, 50; publishes *De Corpore*, 50; attempts to square the circle, 52, 53, 55; attacks the universities, 51-7; controversy with John Wallis, 52-5; becomes a favourite at Court, 58; receives a pension of £100 a year from Charles II., 59; examination and suppression of his writings ordered, 59, 60; his fame abroad, 61; writes a long Latin poem in his eightieth year, 61; publishes *Decameron Physiologicum* in his ninetieth year, 55; produces a work on Common Law, 61; translates the *Iliad* and *Odyssey*, 62; death, 63; starting-point of his philosophical speculations, 73,

74, 84; aim of his philosophy, 84; subject of philosophy, 84; theory of the universe, 72 *seq.*, 80 *seq.*; divergence from Descartes's views, 81-2; theory of logic, 87 *seq.*; physical science, 98 *seq.*; psychology, 109 *seq.*; theology, 144 *seq.*; freewill, 157 *seq.*; political system, 173 *seq.*; his doctrine of motion, 18, 21, 77, 78, 80, 81, 84 *passim*; materialism of his philosophy, 82, 98; philosophical methods, 12, 13; ethical theories, 21; hostility to established beliefs, 75; attitude towards the spiritual authorities, 29-32, 34, 45, 57, 75; heterodox views, 76; comparison of Hobbes with Bacon, 12, 13; resemblance between Hobbes and Herbert Spencer, 73; a great thinker, 1; a born logician, 70; Euclid his type of reasoning, 88; failure as a mathematician, 53; intellectual energy and boldness, 55, 56, 61, 62; personal timidity, 56, 156; shortcomings, 65; contemporary estimate of him, 67; general opposition aroused by his views, 67; his one-sidedness, 71; idiosyncrasies, intellectual and moral, 70; his unemotional nature, 72; dogmatic and aggressive methods, 77; views of love, 132; cynical views of human nature, 139; style, 9, 10, 117; favourite authors, 65; personal attractiveness, 23-4; sincerity of his friendship, 23, 24; personal appearance and habits, 63-4; devotion to music and tennis, 64.

Hobbes, Thomas (father), 3, 4.
—— Mrs. (mother), 3, 4.
—— John (brother), 4.
—— Francis (uncle), 4.

Q

Printed by T. and A. CONSTABLE, Printers to His Majesty,
at the Edinburgh University Press